D1552658

The Harmonies of *The Merchant of Venice*

The Harmonies of
The Merchant of Venice

Lawrence Danson

New Haven and London Yale University Press

1978

Published with assistance from the
Louis Stern Memorial Fund.

Designed by John O. C. McCrillis and set in Baskerville type.
Printed in the United States of America by
Vail-Ballou Press, Inc., Binghamton, New York.

Published in Great Britain, Europe, Africa, and Asia (except Japan) by Yale University Press, Ltd., London. Distributed in Latin America by Kaiman & Polon, Inc., New York City; in Australia and New Zealand by Book & Film Services, Artarmon, N.S.W., Australia; and in Japan by Harper & Row, Publishers, Tokyo Office.

Library of Congress Cataloging in Publication Data

Danson, Lawrence.
The harmonies of The merchant of Venice.

Includes index.
1. Shakespeare, William, 1564-1616. Merchant of Venice. I. Title.
PR2825.D3 822.3'3 77-12008
ISBN 0-300-02167-4

For my parents and my children

"though for myself alone
I would not be ambitious in my wish
To wish myself much better, yet for you,
I would be trebled twenty times myself."

Contents

Acknowledgments

This is a book about a play that deals, among other things, with the difficulties of repaying the debts of love. In the course of writing it I have been sustained by more intelligent advice and generous encouragement than any author could hope to merit: now I undertake the inevitably inadequate requital. I owe a general debt of gratitude to Princeton University, its students, faculty, and, especially, my colleagues in its Department of English. Michael Goldman and Daniel Seltzer read an early draft of the book, and to them I am grateful for a timely warm reception. D. W. Robertson, Jr., and Thomas P. Roche, Jr., also read that early draft: they offered many valuable suggestions, some of which I even had the sense to follow. A. Walton Litz, as Chairman of the Department, has helped throughout. Another good and generous critic to whom I am indebted is my wife, Mimi: she made writing this book possible and worthwhile.

I have used The New Arden edition of the play (ed. John Russell Brown), in some few cases silently altering punctuation for the sake of clarity. For other plays I have used The Riverside Shakespeare (textual ed. G. Blakemore Evans). Biblical quotations, unless otherwise stated, are from The Geneva Bible of 1560, a version with which Shakespeare was certainly familiar.

Introduction: "By two-headed Janus!"

Shakespeare may after all have been master of only a single dramatic genre. The First Folio's tripartite grouping into Comedies, Histories, and Tragedies is sensible, and for most purposes gives a clear enough idea of the landscape. Move up for a closer view, however, and you find that the trees in the forest have a disconcertingly Birnam Wood–like way of shifting from their accustomed places. *Troilus and Cressida,* for instance, although the accidents of the printing-house make it a particularly notorious case, is also an exemplary one. The play never made it into Heminges' and Condell's table of contents. In the Quarto it was called a history, although the writer of the Quarto's dedicatory epistle described it as a comedy; in the Folio, its title page calls it *The Tragedie of Troylus and Cressida.* Subsequent generations, faced with this Polonian multiplication of categories—as well, of course, as with the play's intrinsically recalcitrant form—have taken the reasonable expedient of calling it, simply, a "problem play." And that, I suggest, is what any Shakespearean play becomes when considered curiously enough.

All Shakespeare's plays, then, are problem plays, but some problem plays are more insistently problematic than others. There is, for instance, that group from the middle of Shakespeare's career—*All's Well That Ends Well, Measure for Measure, Troilus and Cressida,* and, by some reckonings, *Hamlet*—which, thanks to a series of distinguished critical studies, has achieved nearly canonical status as "Shakespeare's Problem Plays." [1] But the "problem play"

1. F. S. Boas, *Shakespeare and His Predecessors* (New York, 1905); W. W. Lawrence, *Shakespeare's Problem Comedies* (New York, 1931); E. M. W. Tillyard, *Shakespeare's Problem Plays* (Toronto, 1949).

canon is constantly being revised—such is the nature of the problem. Thus a recent critic considers "the problem plays of Shakespeare" to be *Julius Caesar, Measure for Measure,* and *Antony and Cleopatra.*[2] In one of the most magisterially complete investigations of *Shakespeare and the Traditions of Comedy* the problematic designation is conferred on *The Merchant of Venice, Much Ado About Nothing, All's Well That End Well,* and the ubiquitously problematic *Measure for Measure.*[3]

But we can forgo tabulation. The slightest acquaintance with modern Shakespearean criticism convinces us that there is not one among the thirty-seven plays that is not, quite seriously, a "problem" to some reasonable man or woman. That is one reason books continue to be written about Shakespeare—whole books, even, about individual plays: one person's noble Moor will always be another's ignoble savage.

It is all the more remarkable, then, that *The Merchant of Venice,* the most scandalously problematic of Shakespeare's plays, has never—well, hardly ever—received book-length attention. (Obviously the statement needs qualification, which I will give in due course. But the most glaring exceptions tend only to prove the rule: several books have been devoted to Shylock—his stage history, literary genetics, special pleadings of various sorts; but studies of Shylock are not the same thing as studies of Shakespeare's play.)[4]

2. Ernest Schanzer, *The Problem Plays of Shakespeare* (London, 1963).

3. Leo Salingar (London, 1974). W. H. Auden, *The Dyer's Hand* (New York; Vintage Books ed., 1968), p. 223, calls *MV* "as much a 'problem' play as one by Ibsen or Shaw."

4. On stage history, see Toby Lelyveld, *Shylock on the Stage* (London, 1961). On genetics: Jacob L. Cardozo, *The Contemporary Jew in Elizabethan Drama* (Paris, 1925; rpt. New York, 1955); M. J. Landa, *The Jew in Drama* (London, 1926); Hermann Sinsheimer, *Shylock: The History of a Character* (London, 1947). Bernard Grebanier, *The Truth About Shylock* (New York, 1962), is more difficult to categorize: it is all-too-inclusive, seemingly bent on telling "the truth" about every subject on which the author has formed an opinion. Grebanier relies

Whether this surprising state of affairs exists despite or because of the fact that *The Merchant of Venice* is so notoriously an object of critical contention I do not know. I do know—we all know—that the play is in the very deepest ways a "problem," the only one of Shakespeare's plays, not excepting even the physically gruesome *Titus Andronicus* or the physically and morally unendurable *King Lear,* which a sizeable body of sane people might consider unfit to be seen or read. It is a matter of fact: on March 31, 1974, *The New York Times* still saw the need for a column by a member of its editorial board arguing the case (as the headline put it) "Why Shylock Should Not Be Censored." In England, once upon a time when a civilization different from our own seems still to have flourished, the twelve-year-old Rupert Brooke played the part of Portia in a school production.[5] Today, after the Holocaust, the play no longer seems so obviously suitable for childish renditions.

The book which follows will of course speak for itself. What introduction it needs, especially by way of establishing the anomalous state of criticism regarding *The Merchant of Venice,* can be got at through the article in *The New York Times.* The occasion for the article was the presentation on American television of the National Theatre Company's production, with Laurence Olivier as Shylock and Joan Plowright as Portia. Fred M. Hechinger's argument against censoring the play, despite the sensitivity of some Jewish groups, was made easier because he found in Olivier's performance no simple-minded stereotype but

---

heavily on source-study and literary analogues; but the value is vitiated by his condescending attitude toward the history he records: e.g., "Only once in a while [in Shakespeare] do we come upon a point of view that brings us up short with a reminder that we cannot expect even the greatest of sixteenth-century poets to surmount the limitations of his time in every detail of his thought. One such instance is Antonio's requirement that Shylock become a Christian—*the only moment in the play that throws us back to Shakespeare's day*" (p. 291; my italics).

5. Christopher Hassall, *Rupert Brooke* (London, 1964), p. 30.

rather a Shylock who forced one to "question and reject the stereotypes." Thus, "a modern viewer might discover a Shylock who, though vengeful, had much to be vengeful about." He might discover, too, that Shylock, "though engaged in what was in Elizabethan society considered the disreputable business of money-lending, is in truth no more materialistic than the hedonistic Beautiful People of Belmont, the Gentile Pleasure Palace." Later in his article, Hechinger poses some questions:

> Is it by accident or design that Shakespeare allows the Duke, as representative of Elizabethan propriety, to philosophize about Christian mercy ("Thou shalt see the difference of our spirits") minutes before he sanctions Shylock's unmerciful destruction? Why was Portia, the playgirl of the Elizabethan World, given that line of the ultimate hypocrisy—"The quality of mercy is not strain'd / It droppeth as the gentle rain from heaven"—as a prelude to utterly wiping out Shylock? Could Shakespeare have put in Shylock's mouth that classic assault against discrimination, "Hath not a Jew eyes. . . ." if he wanted merely to create a hateful stereotype?

In the chapters that follow I will, among other things, take up the substance of these rhetorical questions—none of which, incidentally, seems to me to have any very simple answer. What interests me here is that Hechinger's defense of the play is based on the supposition that *The Merchant of Venice* is, at heart, a deeply ironic play condemning the hypocrisy of predatory Christians. And the argument is not a new one; it has become indeed something of a commonplace, one of the major lines modern critics have taken on the play.

Now, in sketching the critical situation I want to avoid drawing the line of opposition too sharply. Critics who disagree about the fundamental intention of the play can nonetheless find many significant things to agree upon.

While I disagree with the direction the article writer takes, I would of course acknowledge that there are many instances of Christian hypocrisy in the play, and that Shakespeare expects us to recognize them. (Shakespeare is always keen in his exposure of hypocrisy, regardless of the hypocrite's race, creed, color, or place of national origin.) But in placing major stress on the faults of the Christian characters, turning Portia, its spokesman for as much doctrinal message as the play carries, into a "playgirl," and its usurious—and potentially murderous—Jew into a representative of "the Jewish work ethic" afflicted with a mere "touch of misanthropy," Hechinger clearly aligns himself with an identifiable tendency in modern criticism of the play.

Where or when that tendency first manifested itself is difficult to say. The play's critical history is closely bound up with its theatrical history; perhaps, then, the ironic tendency in *Merchant*-criticism began as soon as Charles Macklin, in 1741, eschewed a broadly comic Shylock in favor of a horrific one. More likely, though, it is a nineteenth-century product; many of its best exponents clearly show their Romantic predispositions; and credit on the theatrical side should therefore go to Edmund Kean who, in 1814, created the first humanly credible—which is to say, by definition, pitiable—Shylock. It is difficult to know at any historical moment whether the stage is following the critics, or vice versa; both seem unconsciously to cooperate with what we desperately call the spirit of the time. At any rate, Kean is certainly in some measure responsible for the transitional situation Hazlitt reported in 1817: "In proportion as Shylock has ceased to be a popular bugbear 'baited with the rabble's curse,' he becomes a half-favourite with the philosophical part of the audience, who are disposed to think that Jewish revenge is at least as good as Christian injuries." [6]

6. Quoted in the Variorum edition of *MV*, ed. H. H. Furness (Philadelphia, 1888), p. 427.

Hazlitt's appreciation of the character is judicious, certainly by comparison with some Romantic effusions—like Heine's, for instance, which I quote in chapter 4. Very movingly, Hazlitt's remarks show how Shylock's religion, once an overwhelming invitation for distortion from the anti-Semites' side, may in a post-Romantic age lead as easily to a predisposition in his favor:

> There is a strong, quick, and deep sense of justice mixed up with the gall and bitterness of his resentment. The constant apprehension of being burnt alive, plundered, banished, reviled, and trampled on might be supposed to sour the most forbearing nature, and to take something from that "milk of human kindness" with which his persecutors contemplated his indignities. The desire of revenge is almost inseparable from the sense of wrong; and we can hardly help sympathizing with the proud spirit hid beneath his Jewish gaberdine. . . .[7]

With Henry Irving's Shylock (1879) the part became high tragedy, and the play became, in effect, Shylock's play; Irving's Jew still reigned on the stage when Rupert Brooke was essaying with infant voice the speeches of Portia.

Theatrical history is only incidentally a part of my concern in this book; enough has already been said about it, I think, to indicate how much the modern ironic reading of the play is indebted to Romantic and Victorian theatrical example.[8]

The ironic approach has been taken to its furthest extreme by Leslie Fiedler, and by A. D. Moody in his *Shake-*

7. Ibid.

8. On theater history, see (in addition to Lelyveld, *Shylock on the Stage*) John Russell Brown, "The Realization of Shylock: A Theatrical Criticism," *Early Shakespeare,* Stratford-upon-Avon Studies, 3 (London, 1961) : 187–209; and his *Shakespeare's Plays in Performance* (London, 1966), pp. 83–103.

speare: The Merchant of Venice.[9] Moody's book is only sixty-four pages long, including bibliography and index; it is the major qualifier to my equivocal statement that there have been no "book-length" studies of the play. Moody has no doubt that "irony . . . is at the centre of [the play's] meaning." The gist of his argument can be appreciated from an introductory paragraph:

> To emphasise the importance and centrality of the irony, I would suggest that the play is "about" the manner in which the Christians succeed in the world by not practising their ideals of love and mercy; that it is about their exploitation of an assumed unworldliness to gain the worldly advantage over Shylock; and that, finally, it is about the essential likeness of Shylock and his judges, whose triumph is even more a matter of mercenary justice than his would have been. In this view the play does not celebrate the Christian virtues so much as expose their absence.[10]

I perhaps do Moody an injustice by not citing his views in the chapters that follow; to have done so, however, would have turned my book into a running polemic and risked falsifying issues that are by no means black-and-white.

My most fundamental disagreement is over his contention that "The function of the allusions to the Christian ideal is to sharpen our awareness of the human issue, but not to be a measure of it" (p. 13). Moody would have us "look through" the play's Christian-colored spectacles rather than "at" them, in order to see with "definition and depth" the "human issue" (pp. 13–14). But this separation of "human issue" from "Christian ideal" is, however ingenious, a

9. Fiedler, *The Stranger in Shakespeare* (New York, 1972); Moody, *Shakespeare: The Merchant of Venice,* Studies in English Literature, 21, ed. David Daiches (London, 1964).

10. Moody, p. 10. For a similar opinion see H. B. Charlton, *Shakespearian Comedy* (London, 1938; rpt. 1966), pp. 123–60.

patently false distinction. It shows to what shifts the ironist is put to save the play from the embarrassment of its unusually explicit and pervasive scriptural allusiveness.

The dangers of an overly polemical approach are evident from the asterisks Moody sprinkles through the list of "critical writings which have contributed to [his] thinking about the play" (p. 60). The titles Moody pricks out are those he categorizes as "romantic or idealising" (that is, they do not take the play to be *essentially* an exposure of Christian hypocrisy), while the others escape as being sufficiently "ironic." The critical Calvinism behind this bibliographical expedient has its problems. The terminology of the mutually exclusive categories is itself confusing; in my scheme of things, as my remarks about Shylock's theatrical history should make clear, Moody would be one of the play's outstanding "romantic" critics. More importantly, the rigid categorization is insufficiently discriminatory. Sir Arthur Quiller-Couch, for instance, who pronounces Bassanio a "predatory young gentleman," Antonio "the indolent patron of a circle of wasters," Jessica "bad and disloyal, unfilial, a thief"—while he finds that "Shylock is intolerably wronged"—is joint editor of the New Cambridge *Merchant of Venice,* a text "edited and annotated," according to Moody, "in [the 'romantic or idealising'] spirit" (p. 60).

Now no modern Shakespearean would want to be thought deficient in his sense of irony. There is, however, a difference between the critical ironist and the cryptographer, and some of the readings which, outdoing even the Romantic stage tradition, enlist our sympathy exclusively for Shylock do make it seem as though the play were written in cipher. For instance, Harold C. Goddard, in his genuinely interesting chapter on the play, uses the theme of the three caskets as though hidden within it were a skeleton key to the play's secret meanings: "Bassanio is the golden casket. He gained what many men desire: a wealthy wife. . . .

Antonio is the silver casket. He got as much as he deserved: material success and a suicidal melancholy. . . . Portia [because she fails "to be true to her inner self," also] is the golden casket." And Shylock, in "the supreme irony of this ironical play," is "the leaden casket with the spiritual gold within." [11] But it is possible to be respectably ironic without going to a Humpty-Dumpty extreme. Some of the play's best critics, while they are content, for instance, to leave Portia as heroine of the play, are adequately ingenious in searching out those unsettlings of easy expectation and unexamined assumptions—the play's "ironies," that is—which are among the things we value most highly in Shakespeare.

I want to mention some of those critics now without, however, providing anything like a comprehensive bibliographical guide. The intention is still to clarify the general critical situation in regard to the play. Also I hope that in this anticipatory way I can ease part of the impossible burden of acknowledging each point in subsequent pages where my argument makes contact with someone else's, or even where an actual debt has been incurred. The essays I mention are seminal, and with such work it becomes alarmingly difficult to say where we have learned from them afresh or where they have given us back the image of our mind.

I begin with that idiosyncratic pioneer, G. Wilson Knight. Knight's efforts have contributed enormously to the understanding of Shakespeare's symbolic imagery. "Imagery is becoming the very plot itself," [12] he says of *The Merchant of Venice;* and his example has led other critics to see how complexly the ideas of, for instance, music and wealth are woven into the play. His observation that Portia's "riches hold dramatically a spiritual quality," [13] cuts through moun-

11. *The Meaning of Shakespeare* (Chicago, 1951; rpt. 1960), 1 : 86, 92, 112, 101.

12. *The Shakespearian Tempest* (London, 1932), p. 130.

13. *Shakespearian Production* (London, 1964), p. 127.

tains of misleading criticism about the supposed materialism of the play's central pair of lovers. Knight makes connections which, once established, seem too natural ever to have needed connecting: "Love and beauty are regularly in Shakespeare compared to riches; Portia is vitally associated with Christianity; and she is an heiress with an infinite bank-balance. In this play of greed her serene disregard of exact sums is supernal." [14]

The complexly metaphorical nature of the wealth—Antonio's, Portia's, Shylock's—to which Wilson Knight calls attention is the subject of John Russell Brown's chapter on the play: "It may seem *malapropos* to talk about . . . romantic love in terms of buying and selling, leaseholds, merchandise, and bargains, but in each of the early comedies, and in many other plays and poems, Shakespeare wrote of love as of a kind of wealth in which men and women traffic." [15] Critics of all persuasions have been aware of the play's unusually prominent series of binary relationships: Christian and Jew, Belmont and Venice, mercy and justice, and so on. Brown adds to these "the comparison of the two usuries" (p. 65)—that is, Shylock's kind and the kind practiced by the lovers, which resembles the usury described in Sonnet 6: "That is not forbidden usury, / Which happies those that pay the willing loan."

C. L. Barber is another critic who increases our awareness of the interplay between loving prodigality and spiritual meanness. He is aware that the play's various thematic pairs should not be taken simply as stark opposites. Here is

14. Knight, *Shakespearian Production,* p. 128. An attack on Knight in particular, and on so-called "theologizing" critics in general, is mounted by Roland M. Frye, *Shakespeare and Christian Doctrine* (Princeton, 1963); see also Sylvan Barnet, "Some Limitations to a Christian Approach to Shakespeare," *ELH,* 22 (1955) : 81–92. One interesting response is by Paul N. Siegel, *Shakespeare in His Time and Ours* (Notre Dame, 1968), pp. 22–68.

15. *Shakespeare and His Comedies* (London, 1957), pp. 45–81.

his description of the complex relationship of Jew and Christian:

> Shylock is the opposite of what the Christians are; but at the same time he is an embodied irony, troublingly like them. So his role is like that of the scapegoat in many of the primitive rituals which Frazer has made familiar, a figure in whom the evils potential in a social organization are embodied, recognized and enjoyed during a period of licence, and then in due course abused, ridiculed, and expelled.[16]

The fact of similarities between Shylock and the Christians who surround him does not lead Barber to the simplistic—or "ironic"—assumption that exposure of the Christians is what Shakespeare is chiefly up to. "No other comedy, until the late romances," he writes, "ends with so full an expression of harmony as that which we get in the opening of the final scene of *The Merchant of Venice*" (p. 187). That remarkable harmony, which is something both seen and heard in the play's fifth act, is earned by Shakespeare for his characters and the audience; the achievement of it is one of the things my book is about.

I begin with the image of things round or circular—ambiguous images, some of them, but suggestive too of harmonious resolutions. Sigurd Burckhardt, in his provocative essay about the play, also makes the idea of "circularity and circulation" essential to his conception:

> . . . the plot is *circular:* bound in such a way that the instrument of destruction, the bond, turns out to be the source of deliverance. Portia, won through the bond, wins Antonio's release from it; what is more, she wins it, not by breaking the bond, but by submit-

16. *Shakespeare's Festive Comedy* (Princeton, 1959; rpt. Cleveland, 1963), p. 168.

> ting to its rigor more rigorously than even the Jew had thought to do. So seen, one of Shakespeare's apparently most fanciful plots proved to be one of the most exactingly structured; it is what it should be: the play's controlling metaphor. As the subsidiary metaphors of the bond and the ring indicate, *The Merchant* is a play about circularity and circulation; it asks how the vicious circle of the bond's law can be transformed into the ring of love. And it answers: through a literal and unswerving submission to the bond as absolutely binding.[17]

Burckhardt's purposes are different from my own. In Burckhardt's view, the subject of poetry (or drama) is always poetry itself; each poem or play is the allegory of its own creation. The results of this Stevens-like assumption are often splendidly illuminating; they can also, however, be dizzying, since the assumption creates a vortex, the play and its commentary spiraling inward to a point at which nothing exists but the desire of the poem to be written. Precisely the danger of that kind of solipsism is what Burckhardt takes *The Merchant of Venice* to be about; the paradoxical nature of his stance, however, makes it impossible for his essay to avoid the temptation he describes Shakespeare as facing and avoiding in this play.

The Merchant of Venice breaks the circle of self-regarding poetry or drama. There is no contradiction in recognizing a deep fairy tale, wish-fulfillment quality in the play, and simultaneously its honest obedience to the laws of the humanly and socially possible. The negotiation of these two tendencies is a part of the business of all Shakespearean comedy. *The Merchant of Venice,* which seems to be equally about commerce and romance, about hard dealings on the Rialto and music-making on the beautiful mountain, thrusts that characteristically Shakespearean doubleness upon us in

17. *Shakespearean Meanings* (Princeton, 1968), p. 210.

a particularly troublesome way. The decision, conscious or unconscious, of different critics to emphasize either the one tendency or the other accounts in large measure for the Janus-like state of contemporary critical opinion. In my own chapters about the play I try to be mindful of both tendencies (which seem divergent chiefly because of the limitations of our discursive critical vocabulary); and this requires some historical account of those issues, as it were beyond itself, to which the play points, as well as some theoretical consideration of the kind of play it is.

Most central of these considerations, and most controversial, is the fact that the play was written by a Christian for a Christian audience, and that it is about Christian issues. The basic case is made in decisive terms by Frank Kermode:

> *The Merchant of Venice* . . . is "about" judgment, redemption, and mercy; the supersession in human history of the grim four thousand years of unalleviated justice by the era of love and mercy. It begins with usury and corrupt love; it ends with harmony and perfect love. And all the time it tells its audience that this is its subject; only by a determined effort to avoid the obvious can one mistake the theme of *The Merchant of Venice*.[18]

18. "The Mature Comedies," *Early Shakespeare*, Stratford-upon-Avon Studies, 3 (London, 1961): 224. The quotation marks Kermode puts around the word "about" indicate what every critic is aware of, that there will always be some distance between the art object itself and any statement describing it. The practical hope of criticism is that it can achieve some clarifications, and thereby make the experience of the art even richer; but a degree of abstraction is the price of the earned insight. Recently, however, some notable critics have grown restive over that price, which they call "thematics" or "reductionism": see, for instance, Richard Levin, "Some Second Thoughts on Central Themes," *MLR*, 67 (1972): 1–10; "Third Thoughts on Thematics," *MLR*, 70 (1975): 482–96; also Stephen Booth, "On the Value of *Hamlet*," *Rein-*

But of course Kermode is aware that many intelligent writers have found it perfectly easy "to avoid the obvious." A. D. Moody takes Kermode's statement to epitomize "the established view" (p. 9), and then proceeds vigorously to oppose it: "I have to confess that what seems to me obvious, is that the promised supersession of justice by love and mercy does not come about, and that the end is something of a parody of heavenly love and harmony." And so it goes: as I said at the outset, the play is a problem.

In fact there is no single "established view" of the play. And it is worth speculating why the kind of interpretation argued by Kermode, as well as by the critics I will acknowledge below, has not found universal acceptance; why it has met and continues to meet strenuous denials; and why something as "obvious" as Kermode declares it to be has not become the property of the common reader of *The New York Times* Arts and Leisure section. And why, for that matter, did it take so long to be discovered in the first place? As far as I can determine, the first report of the play's specifically Christian allegorical element was delivered in 1916 to the Jewish Historical Society (as with a nice irony it so happens) by Sir Israel Gollancz.[19]

I suspect that the chief reason for opposition to a "Christian reading" (to use, for the moment, a crude shorthand) is the threatening implications it might seem to hold, not just

---

terpretations of Shakespeare, ed. Norman Rabkin (New York, 1969), pp. 137–76 (Booth takes exception to the word "meaning," which has for him the implication of things fixed and formulated, rather than more excitingly active); and most pertinent to my context, see Norman Rabkin, "Meaning and Shakespeare," in *Shakespeare 1971,* ed. Clifford Leech and J. M. R. Margeson (Toronto, 1972), where the attack on "meaning" is carried on specifically with reference to *MV*. Like Booth's, Rabkin's objection is, in part, to the restraints which "rational arguments" place on the reader's or audience's freedom of response.

19. The report of that lecture, and two others, is gathered together as *Allegory and Mysticism in Shakespeare: A Medievalist on "The Merchant of Venice"* (London, 1931).

for *The Merchant of Venice,* but for the rest of the canon as well. Critics are afraid that a "Christian reading" will limit Shakespeare's range of meaning, robbing him of his glorious multivalency and replacing it with rigid dogma. If one values Shakespeare's apparently infinite openness to possibilities, then the idea that he gave allegiance to a determinate set of beliefs may seem to threaten restriction, rather than, as I believe it does, to extend even further the extraordinary range of his dramaturgic vocabulary. Christian doctrine may be held suspect—even by critics who happen themselves to be Christian, for this is not a matter of personal religious convictions—as offering a skeleton key to univocal Shakespearean meanings. And where then is our "myriad-minded" Shakespeare?

Any dogma, even that of our modern antipathy to dogma, is for the artist only a means to an end. Its value to the work of art is determined only partly by the validity of the dogma, and even more by the intelligence, suppleness, and skill of the artist. Marxism, for instance, can produce the most deadly sort of official art; or, in the hands of an artist who can make his doctrine work for his art, it can produce a *Mother Courage.* Christian doctrine similarly is only as useful to the artist as the artist is worthy of that doctrine. Shakespeare's Christianity—and no doubt the allegiance was at least as complex as was Brecht's to Communism—is made by Shakespeare an amplifier, not a deadener, of conceivable meanings.

At least it is in *The Merchant of Venice.* As for the rest of the canon an analogy may help: No one would be particularly ruffled to hear that Shakespeare's history plays contain a serious consideration of the nature of kingship; there would be disagreement about the extent to which his treatment worked finally either to confirm or to question orthodox political doctrine, but that the plays took that doctrine as their starting point could hardly be denied. In discussing the two parts of *Henry IV* one person might want to stress the uncanny vivacity of the *dramatis personae,* the "realism" of Falstaff and the rest; but even so there would be little objection to someone else pointing out a more schematic structure informing the plays and recognizable as a version of Morality dramaturgy, in which Hal is the Prince tempted on various sides by figures representative of false worldly goals. "Banish plump Jack, and banish all the world": the line will read poignantly whichever tendency is stressed, and most poignantly if both are kept simultaneously in mind.

Shakespeare's concern with the idea of kingship is reflected somewhat in *King Lear,* hardly at all in *The Two Gentlemen of Verona;* it appears as an element, although submerged, in *Measure for Measure;* it is there in *The Tempest,* but it is virtually irrelevant to a consideration of *Othello.* And similarly with this matter of Christian doctrine: In *The Merchant of Venice* the relationship of justice to mercy, and the theological vocabulary the theme entails, is strikingly prominent. And so it is too in *Measure for Measure.* In less obvious ways, Christian ideas of justice and mercy figure crucially in *The Tempest;* and those ideas are very much a part of the "problem" of *All's Well That Ends Well.* In the history plays the relation of justice to mercy is treated almost entirely in secular and "realistic" ways. A discussion of *Love's Labor's Lost* or *Twelfth Night* might conceivably involve the question of justice and mercy in a Christian world—but I suspect that the point would seem somewhat forced. It probably would not impinge on a consideration of *The Comedy of Errors.*

The point, simply, is that in some plays Shakespeare may, for whatever artistic reasons, choose to bring forward an aspect of Christian belief and make it a part of his dramatic strategy—as he chooses in some plays to bring forward the myths of kingship. In either case he is drawing upon ideas common to his time. But that is very different from saying that Shakespeare's ideas are common.

Of writers who stress the elements of explicitly Christian

concern in the play, I want to mention two whose importance cannot sufficiently be acknowledged in footnotes. Nevill Coghill, in "The Basis of Shakespearean Comedy," argues eloquently that the play "is a presentation of the theme of justice and mercy, the Old Law and the New." [20] "Seen thus," Coghill writes, "it puts an entirely different complexion upon the conflict of Jew and Gentile. The two principles for which, in Shakespeare's play, respectively they stand are both *inherently right,* and they are only in conflict because, whereas God is absolutely just as He is absolutely merciful, mortal and finite man can only be relatively so, and must arrive at a compromise" (p. 21). Coghill's insistence upon the inherent rightness of both parties to the thematic conflict is crucial: it makes the conflict eternally interesting, rather than merely a matter of an obvious right versus an obvious wrong; and hence, in its full dramatic embodiment, it makes the human characters in that conflict complex, interesting, *alive* both as idea and as person.

But it is not easy to keep the complexity in mind; the vocabulary of simpler oppositions is more native to us. Coghill himself, for instance, speaks of the trial's outcome as showing that "Mercy has *triumphed over* justice" (p. 23, my italics). And Barbara Lewalski, whose article "Biblical Allusion and Allegory in *The Merchant of Venice*" I want, with Coghill's, especially to acknowledge, also says of the trial that "allegorically, the scene develops the sharpest opposition of Old Law and New in terms of their respective theological principles, Justice and Mercy, Righteousness and Faith; it culminates in *the final defeat of the Old Law* and the symbolic conversion of the Jew." [21] Throughout my own discussion, I have tried to keep the idea of *comple-*

20. *Essays and Studies,* 3 (1950): 1–28; a revised version appears in *Shakespeare Criticism, 1935–1960,* ed. Anne Ridler (London, 1963).

21. *SQ,* 13 (1962) : 338; my italics. A substantial article on the exegetical tradition relevant to the play appeared after this book was completed: John S. Coolidge, "Law and Love in *The Merchant of Venice,*" *SQ,* 27 (1976) : 243–63.

tion or *fulfillment,* rather than victory or defeat, the guiding principle.

Finally, I want to suggest another reason why a "Christian reading"—or some version of it—continues to meet resistance. Surely the play is incomprehensible without an understanding of Portia's speech on "The quality of mercy." And yet, despite its almost intolerable familiarity, the speech's plain theological statement can be—frequently, I am sure, is—mistaken or overlooked. When Mr. Hechinger calls its opening lines "the ultimate hypocrisy" he is thinking, probably, of human conduct in a secular world: Portia says we should be nice to each other, but then she seems not to act very nicely (from the secular point of view) toward Shylock. Now of course the play does say a great deal about how we ought to treat our fellow human beings, but it does so in a very particular theological context. It is the context invoked by Isabella, when she argues against Angelo's construction of "the law" in *Measure for Measure:* "Why, all the souls that were were forfeit once, / And He that might the vantage best have took / Found out the remedy" (*MM* 2.2.73–5). Ideas of mercy and justice; of the law—both of God and of man; of the charitable treatment of one's neighbor and of one's enemy: these matters are, in *The Merchant of Venice,* explicitly referred to the unique event of Christ's redemptive sacrifice. The point is so basic to the play's intentions that I have risked, in this introduction and possibly again in chapter 2, laboring the theologically "obvious" for it.

Theology, however, is not my central concern. Shakespeare's play—one I greatly admire—is. And in what follows I have tried to bring to bear on it whatever critical tools seemed appropriate. This book grew out of my teaching of the play: I hope it retains its usefulness for the nonspecialist student. The professional Shakespearean may find in it things that sound either too odd or too familiar: "I do oppose / My patience to his fury."

1

"The Semblance of My Soul" Love and Friendship in *The Merchant of Venice*

The opening dialogue of *The Merchant of Venice* takes us simultaneously inward and outward. In, to a psychologically troubled world ("In sooth I know not why I am so sad"), out, to a busy and dangerous world where great trading ships, "Like signiors and rich burghers on the flood," "do overpeer the petty traffickers." The two movements—the inward and psychological, the outward and public—are closely related: "Your mind is tossing on the ocean." By his imagistic joining of the world's ocean with the ocean of the mind, Salerio (whose explanation this is for the merchant Antonio's mysterious sadness) creates at least a provisional reconciliation of opposing principles. And this reconciliation is delicately premonitory of other achieved harmonies with which *The Merchant of Venice* abounds.

The circle is the play's most frequently repeated figure of harmony. Patens of bright gold, the heavenly spheres in their musical concord: these are some of the glorious rounds to which, in act 5, other less perfect circles, more darkly glimpsed in the course of the play, eventually give way. But because the characters of *The Merchant of Venice* do still wear their muddy vestures of decay—because, that is, the play achieves its vision of immortal harmonies without being unmindful of the conditions of this mortal world—even the traditional symbols of harmony retain, in this dramatic context, all the furies of complexity. And so it is too, but even more, with those other round and golden things, the play's ducats and wedding rings.[1] Little wonder, even if the extraordinary complication of Shylock's Jewishness could be set aside entirely, that this play so crucially about money and marriage should remain, for the critic, among the most vexatious of all Shakespeare's plays.

The major actions of the play reflect in large the circular imagery of the parts. The three delicately interconnected episodes form a series of dramatic paradoxes, in each of which an apparently irresolvable dilemma is revealed at last to be no dilemma at all, as the opposing ends join in a circle of harmony. In the courtroom, where not only the curious laws of Venice but also the fundamental laws of Shakespeare's comic vision are made most nearly explicit, Portia is balked initially in her appeal for mercy. Returning therefore to the law—from Shylock's point of view, returning to it with a vengeance—Portia searches out every jot and tittle, not in order to wrest or overthrow the law but to fulfill it; and the paradoxical result of that rigor is to reveal the spirit of the law inherent in its letter, its mercy in its constraints. And in the two other major actions a similar course is revealed. In Belmont, before the caskets, Portia upholds the letter of her dead father's rigorous law, and the result is the gracious gift of that which her will would freely have chosen. In the episode of the rings, Bassanio *breaks* the letter of his vow, but with this comic

1. The play's final couplet, "Well, while I live I'll fear no other thing / So sore, as keeping safe Nerissa's ring," is the most neatly pointed, funniest, and one of the most significant instances of this Shakespearean comprehensiveness. The "ring" of that line refers to the visible sign of a sacramental union; and it is also a bawdy pun—the bawdy significations of which are necessary to the fulfillment of the word's primary sacramental sense. See E. A. M. Colman, *The Dramatic Use of Bawdy in Shakespeare* (London, 1974), p. 77: "*Thing*, placed at the end of a line, has the chance to reverberate with its anatomical senses, while jokes equating a ring with the female pudendum are fairly numerous in Renaissance literature."

twist: because he has not been faithless to the spiritual content of that vow—the law of love figured by the golden ring—it is revealed that (*mirabile dictu*) the literal sense was not really broken either. In the strange world of *The Merchant of Venice* it becomes possible simultaneously to give and to keep: by giving the ring to "Balthazar" Bassanio pays one debt of love; but by giving it, in the selfsame gesture, to Portia he ensures the ring's return and the closure therefore of another of the play's circles of harmony. In each case, that of the caskets, the trial, and the rings, the antimonies—whether of law versus freedom, justice versus mercy, friendship versus marriage—resolve themselves in a more comprehensive whole.

In my explorations of the play, I shall try to take into account those manifold complications which make the play's putative resolution in harmony a matter of continuing debate. Shylock, of course, is the great stumbling block. The difficulties he presents are integral to the play's meaning and structure—not, as it is sometimes claimed, the result merely of our distance from Shakespeare's ethos. So mindful am I of the problem of Shylock that I intend to approach it only by degrees, beginning these explorations instead with the first apparent disharmony the play presents, the mysterious sadness of the eponymous merchant, Antonio.

The play's opening lines pose something of a riddle. Antonio's sadness, wearisome though he claims it is to all involved, immediately offers an invitation to begin searching for answers:

> In sooth I know not why I am so sad,
> It wearies me, you say it wearies you;
> But how I caught it, found it, or came by it,
> What stuff 'tis made of, whereof it is born,
> I am to learn:
> And such a want-wit sadness makes of me,
> That I have much ado to know myself.

What follows, however—the attempt by Salerio and Solanio to solve the apparent riddle—should warn us to proceed with caution. Salerio and Solanio have not fared well at the hands of critics: "the two bland little gentlemen," C. L. Barber calls them; [2] and the first item in any bill of indictment ought to be their easy confidence that they can clear up the mystery of Antonio's sadness.

It is not only the jingling similarity of their names which makes Salerio and Solanio seem a Venetian Rosencrantz and Guildenstern. They are lightweights, so insubstantial, indeed, that our texts are not even clear about their names —not even clear, in fact, that there are only two of them.[3] Like Rosencrantz and Guildenstern, they meet their friend's emotional distress with the reasonableness of men who have never felt a similar distress. And like their Danish counterparts, they are rebuffed—though rather more gently. Still, Antonio is not a pipe for any fool to play what tune he will; and though their explanations are plausible, we are confronted with Antonio's assertions that they have not plucked the heart out of this sad mystery.

Salerio and Solanio have two tries at explaining Antonio's state. The first is the mercantile "Your mind is tossing on the ocean" (1.1.8): "Believe me, sir, had I such venture forth, / The better part of my affections would / Be with my hopes abroad" (15–17). Their confidence—"But tell not me, I know Antonio / Is sad to think upon his merchandise" (39–40)—is met by Antonio's equally confident denial:

> Believe me no, I thank my fortune for it—
> My ventures are not in one bottom trusted,
> Nor to one place; nor is my whole estate

2. Barber, *Festive Comedy*, p. 181.

3. I follow Brown (Arden edition) and Dover Wilson (New Cambridge) in the assumption that the "Salerino" of Q_2 is an error (possibly scribal), and that this ghostly "Salerino" (or "Salarino") is in fact the same character as "Salerio."

Upon the fortune of this present year:
Therefore my merchandise makes me not sad.
[41–45]

Now if Antonio says his merchandise makes him not sad, then—it would seem—his merchandise makes him not sad. Still, we may find something ominous in that word "fortune," twice repeated in his demurrer: "fortune," the slipperiest of things to thank or trust to; and indeed Antonio is to prove remarkably unlucky in his ventures, despite the canniness with which he has hedged his mercantile bets. Perhaps business worries will not, as Antonio insists, explain his sadness, but business—or, more generally, money—is very much a concern of the play. The whole question of Antonio's peculiar status as a great Venetian merchant, which seems to be left a dangling non sequitur by this first mannered, elegant conversational exchange, is therefore one we shall have to return to.

Love is another concern of the play, and (with business apparently disposed of) it is the next solution proposed for Antonio's melancholy. Says Solanio (with the air of one making a great discovery): "Why then you are in love" (46). Antonio's reply is as nearly rude as any he gives a Christian in the play, the abrupt, unanswerable "Fie, fie!"

There is one further attempt within the scene to explain away Antonio's sadness: Gratiano's "You have too much respect upon the world" (74). Or perhaps this is not so much a third explanation as a summary of the previous two; both the mercantile and the amorous explanations in effect accuse Antonio of having too much concern for the things of this world. They are the thoughts of "worldly choosers." [4]

4. This phrase, so apposite to the concerns of *MV,* does not in fact appear in the play. Rather it occurs in Stephen Gosson's *The School of Abuse,* where it is used to describe a play—one the Puritan Gosson approved of—which he calls "The *Iew.*" That play, Gosson writes, depicts "the greedinesse of worldly chusers, and bloody mindes of Usurers." *The Jew* is not extant; it occupies, however, a position in regard

The reproof sounds especially ironic coming from Gratiano, whose babbling levity, while it places him at an opposite extreme from Antonio, is not the sort of joyful noise unto the Lord commended by the Psalmist. Solanio, Salerio, and Gratiano, with their confident and curiously repetitive explanations for Antonio's sad state, begin to sound like Job's three comforters. Antonio, at any rate, rejects Gratiano's more comprehensive explanation as decisively as he has the previous ones:

> I hold the world but as the world Gratiano,
> A stage, where every man must play a part,
> And mine a sad one.
>
> [77–79]

The terms of Antonio's response here are especially interesting. The idea that all the world's a stage was a poetic commonplace long before Shakespeare began to realize its lively potential. And generally the effect of the trope is to open out fresh imaginative prospects. Here, however, the effect might seem to be the reverse: since Antonio *is* a character in a play, his world indeed merely a stage and his part a sad one, his self-conscious admission of a fictive status appears to rule out any more guessing about his melancholy's motives. His sadness, he seems to be saying, is merely a *donnée,* and there will be no use searching anywhere for its roots except, perhaps, in the literary and dramatic history of the convention of the Melancholy Man.

Or so it might seem. In fact this commonsensical, literary-historical approach—the sort of approach once used (for instance) by E. E. Stoll to explain away any ambiguities in Shylock's character—is no more valid than the psychologizing guesswork indulged in by the play's own characters,

---

to *MV* comparable to that of the *Ur-Hamlet* to *Hamlet:* some scholars that is, assume that the lost play was in fact Shakespeare's source-play. See Brown's discussion, Arden ed., pp. xxix–xxx.

Salerio, Solanio, and Gratiano. The world may be a stage where every man must play a part, but the world of *The Merchant of Venice* is a very special world, governed by laws (dramatic and judicial) as curious as, but not identical with, the laws that govern "the great globe itself." The way to understand the problems raised by Antonio's sadness is to understand the special laws that govern the conditions of dramatic life in *The Merchant of Venice,* and therefore to understand such thoroughly interdependent factors as the play's modes of characterization, the disposition of its fable, and what matters are relevant and what irrelevant to its interpretation.

Of the two explanations offered for Antonio's psychological state, the mercantile would no doubt have seemed to many in Shakespeare's audience an especially plausible one. (Modern audiences have been more attracted to the amorous explanation.) Living at a time when previously unimaginable fortunes were to be made, or suddenly lost, in overseas trade, the Elizabethan audience would easily understand how a man might be sorely weighed down by business worries; and when that man was a *Venetian* merchant —the most splendid embodiment of that boundless wealth available to one who would dare the hazards of such trading—the audience might well be suspicious of his disclaimers. How could such a man, to whom the wealth of the world indeed lay as perilously open as did the golden fleece to the venturesome Jason, *not* be made "sad to think upon his merchandise"?

There were further reasons to be suspicious of Antonio. Elizabethan attitudes towards the idea of a "merchant of Venice" were complex, compounded in part of admiration, in part of jealousy, but also in part of moral disapproval. Antonio, after all, is no bluff Simon Eyre, the honest Englishman whose joyful competence in the gentle craft of shoemaking makes him, Dick Whittington-wise, Lord Mayor of London. A deep suspicion still attached to these merchants, Italian or English, whose fortunes were made less through the sweat of their brow than through the manipulation of money itself. The ambiguity sometimes felt to reside in Shakespeare's title is no mere undergraduate misunderstanding. The Venetian moneylender and the Venetian merchant were not entirely separate in the Elizabethan mind.

By the last decades of the sixteenth century, the basically agrarian economy of the Middle Ages was for all practical purposes a thing of the past. But for just that reason—its retrospective attractiveness, which made the feudal past take on the aspect of a lost and golden innocence—Elizabethans tended to look upon their own economic situation with alarm or even with stern moral disapproval. Great wealth was concentrated in a relatively few hands—as, of course, it always had been; but that wealth was now being organized into monopolies and trading conglomerates to generate more wealth. The old aristocracy found it increasingly unrewarding to live on the proceeds of its lands. Instead, that land was being put out to pawn in order to raise ready cash. Living on credit, with its attendant benefits but also all its anxieties, was becoming the upper class's normal way of life.[5] But for this new economic reality the social theory of the times, which still remained heavily dependent upon medieval doctrine, simply had no place.

Medieval socio-economic theory refused to recognize an economic sphere with rules separable from the rules of religious morality: "Ye can not serue God and riches" (Matt. 6 : 24). And even into the seventeenth century, the incompatibility of "business" (as we might understand the word) and a man's religious duty toward his fellow man was repeatedly urged from pulpit and press. Indeed, as R. H. Tawney puts it, "The practical implications of the social

5. On the economic history that may be relevant to the situation in *MV*, see Lawrence Stone, *The Crisis of the Aristocracy, 1558–1641* (Oxford, 1965), esp. pp. 539–45.

theory of the Middle Ages are stated more clearly in the sixteenth century than even in its zenith, *because they are stated with the emphasis of a creed which is menaced.*"[6] Although Calvinism would provide the creed which could accommodate the strictest Reformation morality along with the machinery of the new economic order, it still seemed to most social thinkers, as it did to Luther himself, that Christian behavior could never be reconciled with a fully emergent capitalism. "It is only after a struggle with established ideas," writes Tawney, "that a new type of economic order is invested with the respectability of the triumphant fact."[7] In England in the 1590s, the new order had arrived, but not the respectability.

We shall see more fully when it comes time to discuss the question of "usury" how wide was the split between economic fact and economic theory. But now, partly in light of the entrenched conservatism of that theory, it is relevant to cite a play from the latter half of the fifteenth century, both as an example of the conservative theoretical attitude towards "merchants" in general and as an analogue to *The Merchant of Venice* in particular. The *Croxton Play of the Sacrament* has a special interest for the history of drama since it is the only extant example of a complete English "miracle play."[8] It has a further claim on our attention since it has at the center of its actions two merchants, one Christian and one Jewish.

The essential kinship of the two merchants, who for all their denominational differences are alike in their fealty to Mammon, is established from the outset of the Croxton play.

6. R. H. Tawney, *Religion and the Rise of Capitalism* (New York, 1926), p. 66; my italics. My discussion is indebted to Tawney's book and also to his lengthy introduction to Wilson's *Discourse* (see note 7, below).

7. Thomas Wilson, *A Discourse Upon Usury* (1572), ed. R. H. Tawney (New York, 1925), p. 105.

8. J. Q. Adams, *Chief Pre-Shakespearean Drama* (Cambridge, Mass., 1924), pp. 243–62.

Aristorius, the Christian, begins with an exuberant geographical survey of his power and wealth, concluding:

And all ys me lent
My well for to worke in thys worlde so wyde.
Me dare they nat dysplese by no condescent,
And who-so doth, he is not able to abyde.
[ll. 41–44; "well" = "will, desire"]

Aristorius' vaunting sentiments are echoed by his "Presbyter," who also however bids Aristorius thank God for his wealth—which Aristorius is happy to do. After Aristorius' speeches, Jonathas the Jew appears, thanking *his* God (called, as the God of the Jews is often called in medieval literature, "Machomet"). Jonathas' speeches closely echo Aristorius', establishing each in his parallel role: Jonathas as "chefe merchante of Jewes" (l. 116) and Aristorius the Christian as "A merchante myghty, of royall araye" (l. 10).

The two are brought together in a business transaction. Jonathas wants to buy a consecrated Host so that he can establish empirical proof of a Christian "heresy." Aristorius reacts to the proposal with righteous indignation; but when he has bargained Jonathas up from twenty pounds to one hundred, he manages to overcome his scruples, steals the wafer from the church, and delivers it to Jonathas and his fellow Jews. The action that follows is a perfect example of the medieval drama's ability to be at once broadly comic and deeply serious. To the increasing consternation of the Jews, they first stab the wafer—and it bleeds; they try to boil it in oil—but it sticks to Jonathas' hand; they nail the wafer to a post in an attempt to free Jonathas' hand—but his hand comes off, still stuck to the Host. The Jews, growing desperate as the Real Presence so disconcertingly manifests itself, throw both hand and Host into a boiling cauldron; and the oil turns to blood. Finally they cast it into an oven; the stage direction reads: "Here the ovyn must ryve asunder, and blede owt at the cranys, and an image appere owt with woundis bledying" (s.d., 632). Christ speaks to the

Jews, who express contrition and pray for mercy. Jonathas' hand is restored to him.

The doctrinal point about the consecrated Host has been made abundantly clear, both to the audience and to the stage Jews, who have, in effect, been made participants in Christ's Passion and beneficiaries of his mercy. The Jews, led by the merchant Jonathas, therefore troop to church where they are gratefully baptised by the Bishop. But what happens to the Christian merchant is of most immediate interest for our purposes. Aristorius is conscience-stricken and joins the Jews and the Bishop at church. There, he confesses the sin of covetousness and asks for penance; and the Bishop responds:

> Now for thys offence that thou hast donne
> Agens the Kyng of Hevyn and Emperour of Hell,
> Euer whyll thou lyvest good dedys for to done
> And neuermore for to bye nor sell.
>
> [ll. 832–35]

The penance—to give up trade entirely—and the assumed irreconcilability of good deeds verses buying and selling are strikingly revelatory of an attitude towards the world's great "merchants." Few businessmen will ever be involved in a literal transaction to sell Christ's body; but whenever they assume (as Aristorius does) that their wealth "ys me lent / My [will] for to worke in thys worlde so wyde," they are not only being presumptuous; their worldly business has led them to disobey the great injunction that fulfills and epitomizes God's law, "Love thy neighbour as thyself" (see, for instance, Rom. 13 : 9, Gal. 5 : 14; derived from Lev. 19 : 18). And this offence, this lack of charity towards one's fellow men, is an offence against Christ: it is, in effect, to participate once more (as Aristorius has done) in his crucifixion. And it is an offence which any merchant, seeking his individual gain at his neighbor's expense, is particularly liable to commit.

Our first glimpse of Antonio, however, may convince us

that he, of all men, is least in danger from the moral precariousness of the mercantile life. We have not only Antonio's own disclaimers; more importantly we are quickly granted an extravagant demonstration of Antonio's unmerchantlike charity or love. (Because I will use the two words frequently, it should be noted that "charity" and "love" were semantically closer in Elizabethan English than they are now. In Alexander Nowell's popular catechism [1570], for instance, the catechumen learns that the last six of the Ten Commandments treat "the duties of mutual *charity or love* among men" [9] (my italics). In *Love's Labor's Lost* Berowne plays upon the possible interchangeability of the two words in his wittily impious allusion to Romans 13 : 10: "For charity itself fulfills the law, / And who can sever love from charity?" [*LLL* 4.3.361–62]. Berowne's quibble depends upon the fact that "charity" has only a single semantic face while "love" has at least two, one spiritual and one carnal. In thinking about the relationship of Antonio and Bassanio, as in reading Elizabethan literature generally, it should be remembered that the severing of "love" from "charity" is a modern linguistic phenomenon.)

Antonio's loving response is made even before he has heard the particulars of Bassanio's request for a loan. If the request is honorable, Antonio says, "be assur'd / My purse, my person, my extremest means / Lie all unlock'd to your occasions" (1.1.137–39). Antonio has said that he counts the world as nothing more than it is, "A stage where every man man play a part, / And mine a sad one" (77–79); but in his response to Bassanio's need we see Antonio's conception of his role more extensively displayed. His use of the world, and all the things of the world, appears to be all unblameworthy; everything he has or can get (for he must borrow in order to meet Bassanio's needs) is at the service of his friend.

9. *A Catechism Written in Latin . . . together with the same catechism translated into English by Thomas Norton,* ed. G. E. Corrie (The Parker Society: Cambridge, 1853), p. 120.

And as the action of the play progresses, that original phrase, "My purse, my person, *my extremest means* / Lie all unlock'd to your occasions," gathers to itself deeper resonance, until the doomed Antonio's plight may bring to mind the words of Christ, "Greater loue then this hathe no man, when any man bestoweth his life for his friends" (John 15 : 13).[10]

Thus Shakespeare plays with his audience's expectations, giving them a merchant who is (apparently) so far from being guilty of a lack of charity that he comes perilously close to completing literally an *imitatio Christi.* But although a man of sorrow, Antonio is in fact no more a "Christ-figure" than is any man who acts with charity. And indeed in this first reversal of ordinary expectations Shakespeare has prepared the way for a further and more subtle reversal. In one extraordinary, vital instance, the imputation of uncharitableness will still come back upon Antonio, but in a way far different from what the comfortable audience would initially have expected. In the trial scene, both Antonio and the audience will be asked to undergo a difficult lesson in what is meant by Christ's fulfilling of the law: "Ye haue heard that it hathe bene said, Thou shalt loue thy neighbour, and hate thine enemies. / But I say vnto you, Loue your enemies" (Matt. 5 : 43–44). Antonio's un-Christlike but quite merchantlike failure involves his fellow merchant, that insidious doppelganger, Shylock.

Antonio's self-righteously unrepentant answer to Shylock at their first appearance together, that "I am as like to call thee [dog] again, / To spet on thee again, to spurn thee too" (1.3.125–26), is shocking to modern ears. No doubt it would have shocked some in Shakespeare's audience; others, familiar with a literature which treated Jews in such a way as to make Shakespeare's creation of Shylock seem remarkably forbearing, might have applauded Antonio's openly expressed hatred. Shakespeare's own judgment on the matter

10. See Gollancz, *Allegory and Mysticism,* pp. 38–39.

is suggested at the start by Antonio's melancholy and confirmed by the lesson of the trial. Critics who search along a naturalistic bias to find the reason for Antonio's sadness generally condemn Antonio's treatment of Shylock without seeing that the two facts—his sadness and his treatment of Shylock—are intimately related. Antonio's melancholy, I suggest, is his emotional response to a moral failure. Elizabethan ideas about the usury Shylock practices complicate the issue but do not alter the fundamental point: that the Christian is obliged equally to hate the sin but *not* the sinner.[11]

The purposeful ambiguity in the play's title, and the numerous felt similarities between Shylock and Antonio—each one, as the play opens, an odd-man-out—help to make the point. The *malice* with which Antonio has, in the past and now, publicly reproved and humiliated Shylock, convicts him of being, in this instance, himself spiritually a "Jew." For, as St. Paul writes, "he is not a Iewe, which is one outwarde: nether is that circumcision, which is outwarde in the flesh: / But he is a Iewe which is one within, & the circumcision is of the heart, in the spirit, not in the letter . . ." (Romans 2 : 28–29). In treating Shylock as he has done, Antonio violates—and has, apparently, repeatedly violated—one of the more difficult spiritual directives given in The Sermon on the Mount: "Iudge not, that ye be not iudged" (Matt. 7 : 1). Later in the play, in Portia's curious courtroom—a place as much for moral instruction as for legal judgment—Antonio and the audience will have an opportunity to render another kind of judgment, one which rejects the flesh desired by the inner "Jew" and accepts instead the spiritual circumcision of the heart.

By the end of the fifth act, characters and audience have been granted intimations of that music of the heavenly spheres which is too fine for our crude mortal perception.

11. Lewalski, "Biblical Allusion," p. 331, cites Matt. 5 : 39, 44–47.

The idea of musical harmony has by then become a dominant metaphor for the play's actions, and the attitudes of the characters to music has become an important means of knowing them. Jessica, a newcomer to the courtly Belmontese society, is uneasy about her own esthetic response: "I am never merry when I hear sweet music" (5.1.69), she confesses to her Christian husband. But Lorenzo, more native to the musical place, takes it upon himself to instruct Jessica: "The reason is your spirits are attentive" (70). Far from showing a lack of responsiveness, the fact that Jessica is not "merry" when she hears the music shows that she has an appropriate listening attitude: she is prepared to "mark the music" (5.1.88), and to hear in it faint echoes of the spiritual music of divine harmony. Jessica's is a norm of appropriate attentiveness against which we can measure the attitudes of other characters—of Bassanio, for instance, who so carefully marks the music when it accompanies his choice of Portia's leaden casket.

At an opposite extreme is the capering Gratiano, whose delight in "mirth and laughter" (1.1.80) overflows into an ugly sort of joy at Shylock's defeat. And Shylock, of course, is clearly identified as an untrustworthy man who "hath no music in himself, / Nor is not moved with concord of sweet sounds" (5.1.83–84). At the trial, Shylock, whose rigid adherence to a literal law rules out the mollifying effects of music, and Gratiano, with his excessive levity, will produce between them a cacophony of lovelessness.

The musical metaphor tells us about Antonio, too. Antonio's melancholy shows that he is out of tune; that despite his spontaneous charity to his beloved Bassanio, his malice towards Shylock—his enemy but therefore, because of his malice, a spiritual kinsman—keeps him from being fully a part of the ideal harmony. But to Portia's challenge at the trial, "What mercy can you render him Antonio," Antonio responds differently than either Gratiano or Shylock. In his response, which goes beyond love of a neighbor to reach as well the love of an enemy, Antonio shows himself to be at last in tune. In his melancholy, Antonio was incapable of fulfilling the Psalmist's injunction to "Sing vnto the Lord a new song" (Ps. 98); but when he extends his love beyond the circle that includes Portia and Bassanio, reaching outwards with charity for Shylock as well, his gesture makes the "new song" of spiritual love.[12]

There is an appropriate dance to be performed to that heavenly music. To see it we will have to return later to the relationship between Portia and Antonio.

Before coming to that matter, however, I want to consider the other explanation beside the mercantile one that has been advanced for Antonio's melancholy. For the opinion that Antonio is in love continues to be widely held, all his "fie, fies" notwithstanding. Not cranks, but some of the play's most eminent interpreters, both academic and theatrical, perceive a homoerotic disturbance as the basis of Antonio's sadness. The National Theatre production, starring Laurence Olivier, is only one of many modern productions that have given currency to the idea that Antonio's affection for Bassanio, now thwarted by Bassanio's interest in Portia, is the cause of his present world-weariness.

The theater is taking its cue in this instance from the play's scholarly interpreters. For instance, E. M. W. Tillyard writes that "Antonio suffers from a self-abnegating passion that quenches the springs of vitality in him and makes him the self-chosen outcast from society. . . . Antonio now sees himself as useless. Before Bassanio left him for Portia, his life had some direction; now it has none." [13] Antonio calls

12. The Geneva Bible glosses "new song" as "some song newly made in token of their wonderful deliuerance by Christ." See the discussion of the "new song" and the "old song," and St. Paul's "new man" and "old man," in D. W. Robertson, Jr., *A Preface to Chaucer* (Princeton, 1962; paperback 1969), pp. 127–29.

13. *Shakespeare's Early Comedies* (London, 1966), p. 199.

himself "a tainted wether of the flock" (4.1.114); and Professor Tillyard remarks: "Annotators seem to have passed over *wether* as if it were a synonym for *ram* or even a mere variation of sheep. But I cannot believe that Shakespeare did not mean us to accept and give full weight to its full significance." This is lexically titillating, but of even greater interest is the rhetoric of Tillyard's conclusion: "I do not think Antonio a study of homosexuality; *but* Shakespeare presented him as essentially a lonely figure, strikingly different from all the sociable folk he has to do with, except Shylock." [14] The force of that "but" implies that Antonio's loneliness and his difference from "all the sociable folk" make him like a homosexual, even if he is not "a study in homosexuality." Thus Antonio's homosexual attachment is made to explain his sadness, and his sadness to prove his homosexuality. The logic (by no means uniquely Tillyard's) is as curious as the implication that loneliness and a striking difference from sociable folk are characteristic of homosexuals.[15]

Now this explanation for Antonio's melancholy seems to

14. Ibid.; my italics. Cf. Ralph Berry, *Shakespeare's Comedies* (Princeton, 1972), p. 130: "A wether, though scarcely any critic seems conscious of this simple fact, is a castrated ram." This is very strange: whatever Antonio's sexual preference he is surely *not* a eunuch. Nor is the lexical "fact" so "simple": the OED's definition of *wether* is less unequivocal in this matter of animal husbandry than are Tillyard and Berry.

15. See also Fiedler, *Stranger in Shakespeare:* in Fiedler's chapter on *MV,* a "Uranian" Antonio is opposed by a "witch" and "liar" (i.e., Portia). Graham Midgley writes that "Antonio is an outsider because he is an unconscious homosexual in a predominantly, and indeed blatantly, heterosexual society." ("*The Merchant of Venice:* A Reconsideration," *Essays in Criticism,* 10 [1960] : 119–33). Of special interest, both because it presents a more temperate expression of this kind of view and because it will be so widely read by students, is Anne Barton's Introduction to the play in The Riverside Shakespeare. Mrs. Barton's argument is too long for quotation here, partly because she so judiciously trims it with phrases like "there is almost a sense" and "nevertheless," and "somehow," and "seem."

me quite wrong: its implied consequences (as I will explain shortly) are not coherent with the play's overall shape and tone. And it is important to stress that this reason, rather than any *a priori* theoretical objection, is the basis for rejecting the psychosexual interpretation: for what is at issue here is not only Antonio's sexual preference, but the nature of Shakespearean characterization. The possible extremes are these: that Antonio, as Shakespeare created him, is merely a bundle of personified dramatic conventions—melancholy, generous, unlucky; or (at another extreme) that he is a psychologically "realistic" character in whom it is proper to discover submerged psychosexual motivations. And the difficult fact—the very heart of this Shakespearean matter—is that Antonio is not wholly the one sort of character or the other, but a richly impure mixture (like the play itself) of both dramatic tendencies. We need to give due weight to all that is uniquely Elizabethan and "conventional" in Antonio's characterization—and that means, among other things, recognizing him as a figure capable of standing for "abstract" ideas, of representing moral qualities. But the necessity to hold on to both sides of Shakespeare's characterizing variousness also makes it important to reaffirm—even in rejecting the idea that Antonio is primarily motivated by a sexual attachment to Bassanio—the character's actual degree of psychological "realism."

It would be supererogatory to stand up for the "felt life" of Shakespeare's characters were it not that some critics, especially of the school of Stoll, have in fact denied it. Thus Leo Kirschbaum, for instance:

> . . . Most of the Christian characters [in *The Merchant of Venice*] are more depictions of values than they are attempts at giving the illusion of substantial dimensionality. To seek psychological depths in them is not only esthetically wrong but dramatically destructive: they are meant to be felt as the not too differen-

> tiated and discrete cells of a single organism, the Christian community.[16]

But in fact, whatever one's approach is to the play, it is absolutely essential that the Christian characters be differentiated. In considering the play under its aspect as a Christian parable, for instance, the distinctions between Antonio and Gratiano prove quite as necessary as those between Antonio and Shylock. And in the theater, certainly, a director will find it deadly to present his Christians as an insubstantial "single organism"—unless, of course, he gives the play over wholly to Shylock, which is precisely what Kirschbaum does not want to do.

The example of the stage gives me the opportunity to show both the plausibility of the idea that Antonio's melancholy is caused by his "loss" of Bassanio, and also to explain my reason for rejecting the idea. Antonio has said that he is not in love: but the actor must ask *how* he says it. Two monosyllabic expletives might seem a slender basis on which to build a character's motivations, but it can be done, and indeed it seems to have been done with great success. John Russell Brown gives the following account of an aspect of Michael Langham's production:

> . . . Antonio's "Fie, fie" in the first scene, when Salerio accuses him of being in love, was forcefully spoken and followed by an emphasizing moment of embarrassed silence, and the description of the parting of Antonio and Bassanio was listened to in such a way that the answering "I think he only loves the world for him" sounded no less than a measured truth. By such means Langham was able to present Antonio's silent figure in Act V as the merchant of Venice who had just given all his wealth in love to Portia; at the end he was left alone on the stage, seated and idly playing

16. *Character and Characterization in Shakespeare* (Detroit, 1962), pp. 10–11.

> with the piece of paper which had given him the irrelevant news that all his argosies were "richly come to harbour. . . ." The treatment of Antonio throughout the play allowed the end to draw strength from the whole.[17]

An Antonio left lonely at the end of the play, an unassimilated element seriously qualifying the fifth act's conclusion, is becoming the theatrical rule. And since this downbeat version is now so familiar, it is worth recalling that it is not the only possible ending. Granville-Barker, for instance, saw it quite differently: "Portia and Bassanio, Antonio, Lorenzo and Jessica must pace off the stage in their stately Venetian way, while Gratiano's harmless ribaldry is tossed to the audience as an epilogue. Then he and Nerissa, now with less dignity than ever to lose, skip quickly after."[18]

Gratiano and Nerissa skipping may be no more satisfying than Antonio moping: I am not prescribing Granville-Barker to future directors. What is crucial to decide, however, is whether those otherwise innocuous "fies" in the first scene should actually lead to Antonio's exclusion and a final dying fall—that is, to irresolution and disquiet; or to the fuller comic resolution suggested by the insistent musicality of act 5.

Now *The Merchant of Venice* is a play in which harmonies are discovered where only discord had seemed possible, and its dominant figure (whether in details of imagery or in the implied shape of the fable as a whole) is the circle, ring, or round. The love of Antonio and Bassanio chimes in that harmonious round, as does the love of Bassanio and Portia. But to suppose a competition between Antonio and Portia introduces a discord more intractable

17. John Russell Brown, "Three Directors," *Shakespeare Survey*, 14 (1961): 135.

18. Harley Granville-Barker, *Prefaces to Shakespeare* (Princeton, 1946), 1 : 364.

to resolution than that of Shylock, the unmusical man, himself. So it is not the realism nor the humanness, but the consequent introduction of this irreconcilable competition, that leads me to reject the psychosexual explanation for Antonio's sadness.

Although marriage and male-bonding are usually antagonistic principles, they are not necessarily at odds in the world of Shakespeare's comedies. In *Much Ado About Nothing,* it is true, Beatrice's challenge to Benedick, "Kill Claudio," is as decisive a statement of the primacy of heterosexual love over male friendship as one could want —although even here the issue is complicated by our knowledge that Claudio *is* in the wrong. In *The Two Gentlemen of Verona* male friendship seems to be scandalously elevated above heterosexual love.[19] But if forced to choose the Shakespearean "ideal," I should say it emerges most clearly in *The Winter's Tale,* where marriage and friendship are not mutually exclusive but rather mutually dependent. Leontes' sexual possessiveness destroys both his love for Hermione and for Polixenes; and only when friendship has been restored between the men can the play's other restorations take place, including that of Hermione to Leontes. In its treatment of friendship and wedded love, *The Merchant of Venice* is closest in spirit to *The Winter's Tale.*

It is conceivable, I suppose, that one could have a homosexual Antonio without any consequent irreconcilability between Bassanio's two lovers. But then, of course, Antonio's sadness remains inexplicable. And in critical practice, a competition between Portia and Antonio seems the inevitable result of the assumption. According to one account, for instance, friendship is relegated "to a subordinate place" by the end of the play, and Antonio is taught that "there is

19. See R. G. Hunter, *Shakespeare and the Comedy of Forgiveness* (New York, 1965) for a discussion of the *Two Gentlemen* problem. Hunter does not discuss *MV,* but much of what he says about other plays is instructive for this one.

room for friendship within the house of love, but love holds the upper and controlling hand."[20] This shrewish love, however, conflicts with all that Portia says about the nature of her relationship to Bassanio when he wins her in the casket test, when "her gentle spirit / Commits itself to [his] to be directed, / As from her lord, her governor, her king" (3.2.163–65). And it conflicts with the actual result of the ring episode, which is (in part) the reaffirmation of Antonio's loving loyalty to both Bassanio and Portia:

> I once did lend my body for his wealth,
> Which but for him that had your husband's ring
> Had quite miscarried. I dare be bound again,
> My soul upon the forfeit, that your lord
> Will never more break faith advisedly.
>
> [5.1.249–53]

The love of Antonio and Bassanio (whether or not it dares to speak its name) is a textual fact; but a sexual competition between Antonio and Portia is not, and to invent one raises more problems of interpretation than it solves.

Let us return to the first scene, to Salerio and Solanio, and notice a peculiarity of Antonio's rhetoric in his opening speech: more even than the fact of his sadness, Antonio stresses here his own lack of self-knowledge. He knows not why he is so sad; he is "to learn" the origin and composition of his affliction; he is made a "want-wit" by it; and finally, "I have much ado to know myself."[21]

Antonio's echo of the oracular *nosce teipsum* is neither fortuitous nor lightly intended. Lack of self-knowledge is

20. Anne Barton, in The Riverside Shakespeare (Boston, 1974), p. 253.

21. D. J. Palmer, "*The Merchant of Venice,* or The Importance of Being Earnest," *Shakespearian Comedy,* Stratford-upon-Avon Studies, 14 (1972) : 103: ". . . critics who try like Salerio and Solanio to discover the cause of [Antonio's] sadness are wilfully ignoring its dramatic point: 'In sooth, I *know not* why I am so sad.'"

itself at least a part of Antonio's discomfort, and his acquisition of self-knowledge is to be an important aspect of the play which bears his title as its title. But the opening lines only hint at this, leaving the audience to assume that what Antonio is "to learn"—that thing he ominously calls his "fortune"—must portend him ill. We share Antonio's lack of knowledge; our minds, like his, misgive some consequence yet hanging in the still undisclosed dramatic shape of the play. That the real enemy lies as much within Antonio as without we have still to discover.

The melancholy hints afforded by Antonio's prophetic soul are the first of several disturbing elements, counterpointing other elements of gaiety and joyful expectation, which give the play's first two scenes their special character—until, at the beginning of scene three, we have our first real intimation of the cause of Antonio's melancholy when we are brought up short by the confrontation of Antonio and Shylock. It is in the context of these counterpointing tendencies—Antonio's melancholy with its hints of disasters to come, versus, for instance, Bassanio's eagerness to begin the quest of love—that the diagnoses of Salerio and Solanio have their dramatic relevance. These Venetians may be lightweights, but they are well-spoken; and in the first scene they give us, even if unwittingly, further hints at the sort of potentially dangerous world we are entering. The rhetorical ornateness of their speeches, although it may help convict them of emotional superficiality, is entirely to the point. The hazards awaiting in *The Merchant of Venice* first appear to us couched in poetry whose splendor partially mitigates those very hazards. We are simultaneously aware of the dangers the speeches describe, and reassured by the ordered loveliness of the expression.

In Salerio's first speech, the ocean upon which Antonio's mind is supposed to be tossing is a richly sociable place seen from the vantage of a privileged class. Antonio's fleet, like the man himself, is the observed of all observers—

There where your argosies with portly sail
Like signiors and rich burghers on the flood,
Or as it were the pageants of the sea,
Do overpeer the petty traffickers
That cur'sy to them (do them reverence)
As they fly by them with their woven wings.
[1.1.9–14]

The stately bulk of Antonio's "argosies" is attractively set off by the airy lightness of the "petty" vessels playfully doing them homage. Salerio's "Or as it were" introduces a specifically theatrical metaphor, and does so in a markedly artful way. Antonio's ships are likened to the elaborate constructions, called "pageants," used in civic shows, sometimes on the Thames itself: they are the quintessence of Elizabethan magnificence. The portly, self-satisfied ships thus become painted ships upon a painted sea, so that the dangers awaiting them are contained and controlled with a reassuring artifice.

This counterpointing of tone and content is continued as Solanio elaborates his friend's surmise. His "I should be still / Plucking the grass to know where sits the wind" (17–18) is a curiously pastoral mode of entrepreneurial anxiety, for instance; and "piring" (or the Folio's "peering") "in maps for ports, and piers and roads" (19), with its marked rhythm and jingling alliteration, calls attention to itself as comfortable poetry as much as to the unhappy state it describes. In these speeches the potential dangers are emphasized by the wealth of what is threatened, but that wealth has a reciprocally soothing effect, leaving the audience uneasily suspended between confidence and menace. The whole description of mercantile precariousness has a domesticity about it that we would expect to find only in the very best of homes: we hear of the merchant cooling his broth and watching the hourglass—but being reminded by it that his "wealthy" ship may be "dock'd in sand" (27);

of his going to church, but with visions of that mere touch to his "gentle vessel's side" which "would scatter all her spices on the stream" (33). The idea of the spiced stream and of roaring waters enrobed with silks (34) nicely sums up the oxymoronic quality of the entire interlude. On which side, whether on that of the implied confidence or of the menace, the play will finally come down is part of what Antonio is "to learn."

"In Belmont is a lady richly left, / And she is fair, and (fairer than that word), / Of wondrous virtues" (1.1.161–63): in the very rhythms of its presentation the idea of Portia is made to seem a welcome release from an emotional impasse. For as pretty as are the speeches of Salerio and Solanio, their partial inconsequence and their very ornateness impart a heavy, time stopping quality to scene one. Bassanio's embarrassed and long-winded request for a loan similarly has a retarding effect. Now, with the description of Portia, Bassanio introduces a new emotional impetus, giving an exciting alternative to the lugubriousness of Antonio's inexplicable melancholy. And far from revealing himself as a fortune hunter, the "predatory young gentleman" of Quiller-Couch's description,[22] Bassanio shows an entirely appropriate regard for moral priorities. Portia's wealth is mentioned first but quickly and almost by the way; her beauty is mentioned next, with heavier stress; and finally her virtue—fairer than that word "fair" itself. The accelerating rhythm of the progression seems to push the scene forward, striving to reach beyond the boundaries of this scene into the next, into that Belmont we as audience are privileged to reach even before the new Jason.

The transition to scene two satisfies the expectations aroused in scene one and suddenly crystallized in its con-

22. Introduction to the New Cambridge edition, p. xxv. The imputation—quite groundless, I think—that Bassanio is a mere fortune hunter is found in most "ironic" readings of the play.

cluding speeches; but the *weariness* expressed in Portia's initial line is also a complication and, potentially at least, a disappointment. What we discover, then, in the movement of these two scenes is further counterpointing: in the speeches of Solanio and Salerio we found comfort and menace; now, in the larger rhythms of scenic construction we again find counterpointing emotions. The appearance of Portia, so soon after our introduction to the idea of her, satisfies expectation and promises fulfillment and joy, while at the same time the tones of weary, only partially explicable sadness continue as a constant base note.

Scene two, although at first it seems to resolve the impasse of scene one, is in some ways a reprise of that first scene. Here, Portia and Nerissa themselves take parts that correspond to those of Solanio and Salerio; their opening speeches, although in prose, are also mannered and sententious, and while they give us important information, they are also, in a way, time killers. As Portia goes on about the difficulty of following one's own moral precepts and about the impetuousness of youth, and as she describes her various suitors, the sense of excited expectation with which we entered the scene dissipates. We relapse into the retarding wordiness that characterizes scene one—and that created the expectation of release in the first place. But in much the same way as scene one suddenly leapt alive when indefinite longing became crystallized in a name: "In Belmont is a lady richly left. . . . Her name is Portia"—so also this second scene recovers the sense of excitement with an act of naming:

> *Nerissa.* Do you not remember lady in your father's time, a Venetian (a scholar and a soldier) that came hither in company of the Marquis of Montferrat?
>
> *Portia.* Yes, yes, it was Bassanio, as I think so he was call'd.
>
> [1.2.108–11]

It remains for Portia in this scene to cope with the business of the Prince of Morocco. But surely it is her "Yes, yes, it was Bassanio," that rings most clearly for us. Thus both scene one and scene two resolve themselves on notes of expectancy and striving together, as Bassanio names Portia and Portia names Bassanio. The scenes thus seem to reach out towards each other in the promise of union between Venice and Belmont—until, with remarkable artistry, the complication of Shylock is sprung suddenly upon us with the first words of scene three.

Perhaps the most surprising aspect of the similarity between the first two scenes is the complex of relationships it intimates between Antonio and Portia. And because these relationships are especially significant for the sense of the play as a whole, as well as for the problem of Antonio's mysterious sadness, it is a matter worth pausing over. Everyone will have noticed the way in which their opening lines complement one another: Antonio's "In sooth I know not why I am so sad," and Portia's "By my troth Nerissa, my little body is aweary of this great world." And while the source of Portia's uneasiness is more specifically indicated than Antonio's, she too is a character who has yet "to learn."

There are other similarities. Each appears at first as a masterful character—rich, intelligent, the center of his or her little world. But these two controlling characters also share an especially acute sense of their lack of ultimate control; in their sadness both Antonio and Portia seem more self-consciously aware than the other characters that they are subject to the vicissitudes of Fortune. Portia is more explicit about this limiting force beyond her control, as she is more aware of the source of her body's weariness: "O me, the word 'choose'! I may neither choose who I would, nor refuse who I dislike, so is the will of a living daughter curb'd by the will of a dead father: is it not hard, Nerissa, that I cannot choose one, nor refuse none?" (1.2.22–26). In the case of Antonio, this sense is more vaguely intimated by his knowledge that there are forces and causes at work of which he is still "to learn."

And indeed this question of having things to learn is very closely bound up with the feeling of being limited in one's powers to choose or act. Again, it is Portia who picks up the hints begun by Antonio and develops them towards explicitness. Her talk about learning and teaching gains point from Antonio's earlier confessed lack of self-knowledge:

> If to do were as easy as to know what were good to do, chapels had been churches, and poor men's cottages princes' palaces,—it is a good divine that follows his own instructions,—I can easier teach twenty what were good to be done, than be one of the twenty to follow mine own teaching: the brain may devise laws for the blood, but a hot temper leaps o'er a cold decree, —such a hare is madness the youth, to skip o'er the meshes of good counsel the cripple. [1.2.12–20]

It would be easy to dismiss these "good sentences, and well pronounced" (1.2.10) as the time wasting chatter Portia herself implies they are. In the rhythms of the first two scenes their apparent idleness does, as we have seen, contribute to the sense that we are being retarded from more important business ahead. But it is worth noticing that Portia's opposition of old laws and youthful freedom, "a cold decree" versus "a hot temper," is our introduction to a dialectic that will be developed, not only in the trial scene, but in the shape of the play as a whole. And the idea that a learner—like Portia or, by implication, like Antonio—may also be a teacher will emerge again, most beautifully and subtly, at the trial. Though Shylock can turn upon the Christians with his threat, "The villainy you *teach* me I will execute, and it shall go hard but I will better the *instruction*" (3.1.65–66), Portia, with her simple didactic question, "What mercy can you render him, Antonio?" (4.1.374), will show how different a lesson can be taken from this ordeal.

The similarities between Portia and Antonio—the central place each occupies in Belmont or Venice, their shared sense of a limitation on their freedom to control their destinies, their knowledge that they are mere learners in the world—are only implicit in the first scenes. Later Portia makes the association explicit; and indeed she goes further, to establish a virtual spiritual identity between herself and Antonio. And she does this in a way so remarkable that we must either dismiss it as elaborate sophistry or seriously entertain it as belonging to a realm beyond that of ordinary experience. For as the means to the identity between herself and Antonio, Portia uses Bassanio as a necessary *tertium quid.*

The place is act 3. Antonio, at the end of the third scene, has given himself up for lost; indeed he summarizes in apparently unanswerable fashion the strongest part of Shylock's argument, the inviolability of "a cold decree":

> The duke cannot deny the course of law:
> For the commodity that strangers have
> With us in Venice, if it be denied,
> Will much impeach the justice of the state,
> Since that the trade and profit of the city
> Consisteth of all nations.
>
> [3.3.26–31]

Then comes one of those moments which, because of the evident emotional burden behind it, has been used by some critics to make of Antonio a competitor against Portia for Bassanio's love:

> These griefs and losses have so bated me
> That I shall hardly spare a pound of flesh
> To-morrow, to my bloody creditor.

Well, gaoler, on,—pray God Bassanio come
To see me pay his debt, and then I care not.

[3.3.32–36]

The transition from this to the next scene is done with the perfect sense of scenic juxtaposition we have observed in the play's first two scenes. As Antonio goes off despairing, with only the wish that Bassanio may come in time to see him once again, Portia enters with others of the Belmont party; and Lorenzo, as the scene opens, speaks of friendship and offers Portia a compliment:

Madam, although I speak it in your presence,
You have a noble and a true conceit
Of god-like amity, which appears most strongly
In bearing thus the absence of your lord.
But if you knew to whom you show this honour,
How true a gentleman you send relief,
How dear a lover of my lord your husband,
I know you would be prouder of the work
Than customary bounty can enforce you.

[3.4.1–9]

It is difficult to believe that Portia's "true conceit / Of god-like amity" includes (as has been suggested) the desire to demote Antonio from his station as "How dear a lover." Irony, like subconscious motivation, is usually more difficult to disprove than to suspect; here we can certainly say that if there is the slightest irony Lorenzo himself is unaware of it. But I do not think the speech is ironic, unless it is the extremely subtle irony of Lorenzo's repeatedly stressing the fact that Antonio is unknown to Portia. For in Portia's response comes the remarkable assertion of her identity, through Bassanio, with the otherwise unknown Antonio:

I never did repent for doing good,
Nor shall not now: for in companions

That do converse and waste the time together,
Whose souls do bear an egall yoke of love,
There must be needs a like proportion
Of lineaments, of manners, and of spirit;
Which makes me think that this Antonio,
Being the bosom lover of my lord,
Must needs be like my lord. If it be so,
How little is the cost I have bestowed
In purchasing the semblance of my soul
From out the state of hellish cruelty!—
This comes too near the praising of myself. . . .

[3.4.10–22]

Thus, according to Portia, Bassanio and Antonio (friends "whose souls do bear an egall yoke of love") must be virtually identical in inward and in outward form; and since Bassanio is Portia's soul, Antonio must also be "the semblance of [Portia's] soul." The exchange of selves between Portia and Bassanio, establishing *their* spiritual identity, is first heard of in Portia's notorious slip of the tongue:

Beshrew your eyes,
They have o'erlook'd me and divided me,
One half of me is yours, the other half yours,—
Mine own I would say: but if mine then yours,
And so all yours. . . .

[3.2.14–18]

Almost despite her conscious will, Portia cannot maintain herself in a "divided" state; her tongue balks at it, and so in giving herself she is reunited *with* herself, "all" Bassanio's. And in her speech in 3.4, responding to Lorenzo, Portia extends this act of giving in order to remain whole until it includes Antonio within the circle of mutual exchange.[23]

23. See the excellent discussion by Alexander Leggatt, *Shakespeare's Comedy of Love* (London, 1974), esp. pp. 147–48.

I said that we would either have to dismiss Portia's speech as sophistry or entertain its serious implications. In other contexts there might be good reason to discount the speech, if not quite as sophistry then at least as a mere poetic commonplace. For the exchange of selves in love is a common trope, and is frequently little more than an ornamental exercise in wit. In *The Two Gentlemen of Verona,* for instance, there is Valentine's pretty conceit,

> To die is to be banish'd from myself,
> And Silvia is myself: banish'd from her
> Is self from self, a deadly banishment!
>
> [3.1.171–73]

At its best, however, the idea—that in giving themselves the lovers become one, so that giving is gaining—can be made to ring startling changes, as it is in the ironic sonnet 42, for instance, and in the mystical union of *The Phoenix and the Turtle.* What distinguishes Portia's use of the trope is the extent to which it is integral with the entire plot: not a conventional love phrase, however beautiful, but an essential aspect of the play's central theme of charity or love. And especially important in that theme is the further complication she adds to the trope, the triple unity that includes herself, Bassanio, and Antonio.

The gift of self is only one instance—although, to be sure, the supreme one—of *giving* in the play. From Antonio's "loan" to Bassanio at the beginning, through the "manna" that Portia, in the final scene, drops in the way of the starving Lorenzo and Jessica (5.1.293–94), and even including, by way of grim contrast, Shylock's "kind . . . offer" of three thousand ducats, the play elaborately illustrates various modes of giving. Some of the instances of giving are comic or ironic. Portia, for instance, describes her Scottish suitor's "neighbourly charity": "He borrowed a box of the ear of the Englishman, and swore he would pay him again when he was able: I think the Frenchman became his surety, and seal'd under for another" (1.2.75–79). Lancelot Gobbo, meeting with his unsuspecting blind father, insists upon being called "Master Launcelot," although old Gobbo protests that he is "No 'master' sir, but a poor man's son" (2.2.48); partly in continuation of the satire on Launcelot's social pretensions, but partly too to show that even a simple gift can make up "the very defect of the matter" (2.2.136), father and son present Bassanio with "a dish of doves"—and in return Launcelot becomes "the follower of so poor a gentleman" as Bassanio. The comedy of the rings in the fifth act—the rings that are both given away and not given away—belongs in this list. But at least one instance of giving is more deeply ambiguous in both its moral and dramatic intentions: Jessica's stealing from her father in order to give to Lorenzo, and squandering the ring Shylock had of Leah when a bachelor, are actions that trouble the mind, and will have to be confronted as we proceed.

Shakespeare's concern with the varieties of giving reveals a peculiarly Elizabethan preoccupation. The punctilious men of the English Renaissance made a fine art of charity; and one of the most influential texts on the subject—one with which Shakespeare would certainly have been familiar—was Seneca's *De Beneficiis.* According to Seneca, the conferring of benefits (a comprehensive term that includes gift giving of all sorts) is a "practice that constitutes the chief bond of human society" (*quae maxime humanum societatem alligat*).[24] It is a social bond because, properly understood, the art has three equally necessary branches: "We need to be taught to give willingly, to receive willingly, to return willingly." The initial giving and the reciprocal returning must be free and spontaneous; benefits, properly understood, are "not investments, but gifts. The man who, when he gives, has any thought of repayment deserves to be deceived" (p. 7). But while one gives with no thought to re-

24. John W. Basore, trans., *The Moral Essays,* Loeb Library ed. (London, 1935), 3 : 18–19.

payment, yet "a benefit passing in its course from hand to hand returns nevertheless to the giver; the beauty of the whole is destroyed if the course is anywhere broken, and it has most beauty if it is continuous and maintains an uninterrupted succession" (p. 15).

The Senecan spirit of openness in giving is clearly present in Antonio's response to Bassanio's needs: "My purse, my person, my extremest means / Lie all unlock'd to your occasions" (1.1.138–39). And his gentle reproof of the long-windedness of Bassanio's request should be understood in the same spirit:

> You know me well, and herein spend but time
> To wind about my love with circumstance.
> And out of doubt you do me now more wrong
> In making question of my uttermost
> Than if you had made waste of all I have:
> Then do but say to me what I should do
> That in your knowledge may by me be done,
> And I am prest unto it.
>
> [1.1.153–60]

Portia's long speech when she gives herself and all that is hers to Bassanio is especially relevant in this context. She frankly acknowledges that with herself there come also her riches, and she wishes indeed that she could therefore be "ten thousand times more rich" (3.2.154). But far from convicting either herself or Bassanio of crass materialism, Portia shows in this her awareness of "benefits" as the chief human bond that Seneca terms them:

> You see me, Lord Bassanio, where I stand,
> Such as I am; though for myself alone
> I would not be ambitious in my wish
> To wish myself much better, yet for you,
> I would be trebled twenty times myself,
> A thousand times more fair, ten thousand times more rich,
> That only to stand high in your account,

I might in virtues, beauties, livings, friends
Exceed account: but the full sum of me
Is sum of something: which to term in gross,
Is an unlesson'd girl, unschool'd, unpractised,
Happy in this, she is not yet so old
But she may learn: happier than this,
She is not bred so dull but she can learn;
Happiest of all, is that her gentle spirit
Commits itself to yours to be directed,
As from her lord, her governor, her king.
Myself, and what is mine, to you and yours
Is now converted.

[3.2.149–67]

It is significant that at the moment of this supreme gift-giving Portia should invoke such explicitly social terms: Bassanio is to be "her lord, her governor, her king." This private exchange of selves and goods thus becomes a model for all others, including those upon which depend the proper ordering of an entire kingdom.

Portia's insistence upon her ignorance is also significant—and the gravity of the situation prevents the modest disclaimer from falling into the merely coy. Bassanio, in addition to all his other newly acquired governing roles, must now become moral tutor to this apt and eager but "unschool'd girl." Portia's entire speech is in this regard gently ironic: the character who here confesses her need "to be directed" is, in that very confession of ignorance, *teaching* central lessons about wedded love, social harmony, the proper giving, receiving, and returning of benefits.

Seneca, in the course of his almost painfully thorough elaboration of the tripartite nature of benefits, touches somewhat grudgingly on the allegorical figures known as the Three Graces. As far as Seneca is concerned, the precise interpretation of the allegory is not a matter of great importance; noting that the poets offer differing accounts of the allegory, Seneca impatiently bids us "accept as true whichever you like," since the only vital lesson to hold onto is just "to give willingly, to receive willingly, to return willingly" (pp. 13, 19). But out of the entire treatise, these by-the-way remarks about the Three Graces, made by Seneca merely for the sake of completeness, were to become the most influential and widely known part of all. The iconography of the Three Graces, already elaborately developed by painters, poets, and moralists before Seneca, was to become, through Seneca, a subject of continuing interest for the Renaissance. Edgar Wind's account of the relevant portion of Seneca's treatise is worth quoting:

> "Why the Graces are three, why they are sisters, why they interlace their hands," all that is explained in *De beneficiis* by the triple rhythm of generosity, which consists of giving, accepting, and returning. As *gratias agere* means "to return thanks," the three phases must be interlocked in a dance as are the Graces *(ille consertis manibus in se redeuntium chorus*); for "the order of the benefit requires that it be given away by the hand but return to the giver," and although "there is a higher dignity in the one that gives," the circle must never be interrupted.[25]

Professor Wind writes of "the ubiquity of Seneca's graces," and cites, from English literature, *The Faerie Queene* VI.x.24, and the gloss to the Aprill eclogue of *The Shepherd's Calendar*. To this I would add an instance from Shakespeare: the interlocking triune dance of generosity forms one of the rings of *The Merchant of Venice*.

We should not expect to find the precise pictorial iconography of a Raphael; nor need we be much worried even by changes in the dancers' sex. Shakespeare is faithful to Seneca in keeping only what is essential—the "triple rhythm of generosity" in its circular dance—and turning that to his own dramatic uses. At moments it is possible to distinguish the

25. *Pagan Mysteries of the Renaissance* (London, rev. ed. 1968), p. 28.

figures in the dance: Antonio first gives, Bassanio receives, and Portia (in the courtroom, and again with her mysterious news that Antonio's "argosies / Are richly come to harbour suddenly" [5.1.276–77]) returns the benefit. But at any particular moment, the movement of the whole may be found implicit in the part. Thus, for instance, Bassanio, having read the "gentle scroll" in the lead casket, kisses Portia and says, "I come by note to give, and to receive" (3.2.140)—a line we may recall later when Portia teaches that mercy "blesseth him that gives, and him that takes" (4.1.183). In the courtroom, Antonio takes from Portia (and the Duke) the gift of Shylock's estate, and in his next gesture offers to redeliver it to Shylock so that ultimately it may go to Lorenzo and Jessica.

Part of the elaborate comedy of the wedding rings finds its significance in the gracious dance: Portia has given Bassanio a ring which Bassanio has now given away—and Portia, who says that she "will become as liberal as" Bassanio (5.1.226), now returns the ring to him. That the third figure in this exchange, the supposed lawyer "Balthazar," is in fact Portia herself adds point: the three dancers in the round of generosity merge into two, finally to lose all distinction through the exchange of selves, confirmed in the marriage ring. Nor is Antonio, although unwived, excluded from this last movement of the dance, for Portia has found in his generous spirit, through Bassanio's "like proportion," the semblance of her own soul.

2

"The Quality of Mercy" The Dilemmas of Divine Law in *The Merchant of Venice*

In Seneca's *De Beneficiis* the bestowing of benefits—that is, in the broadest sense, charity or love—is a civic and humane obligation. But in the specifically Christian context in which the essay came to be so widely read, it is more. For the first Sunday in Advent—the beginning of the Christian year—the Elizabethan Book of Common Prayer appoints the reading of Romans 13 : 8–14, which begins with St. Paul's epitome of the Law:

> Owe no man anything, but to love one another: for he that loveth another hath fulfilled the law. For this, Thou shalt not commit adultery, Thou shalt not kill, Thou shalt not steal, Thou shalt not bear false witness, Thou shalt not covet; and if there be any other commandment, it is briefly comprehended in this saying, Thou shalt love thy neighbour as thyself. Love worketh no ill to his neighbour; therefore love is the fulfilling of the law [cf. Gal. 5 : 14; quoted from *BCP*.]

In the one phrase—"Love is the fulfilling of the law"—there is contained the essence of the Christian's relation to his fellow man and to God. God's love to man is manifest in the gift of his Son, who undergoes in his own person the rigor of the Law and through his sacrifice frees mankind from bondage to the flesh, establishing the New Law of the spirit through which man can attain salvation. Mankind returns the benefit in the only way he can, by imitating divinity through his own love for his neighbor.

From St. Paul's urgent perspective ("The night is past, & the day is at hand: let vs therefore cast away the workes of darkenes, and let vs put on the armour of light," [Rom. 13 : 12]) the doctrine is radically simple. Paul declares the Christian free from the dead letter of the Old Law: "For sinne shal not haue dominion ouer you: for ye are not vnder the Law, but vnder grace" (Rom. 6 : 14). The law pertains to the flesh, but the spiritual Christian is "dead also to the Law by the bodie of Christ" (Rom. 7 : 4), and now, "deliuered from the Law, being dead vnto it" the believer in Christ serves "in newnes of Spirit, and not in the oldenes of the letter" (Rom. 7 : 6).

From other perspectives, however, complications arise. For instance, what is the Christian who has been freed from bondage to the law to make of Christ's assertion in the Sermon on the Mount that not one jot or tittle of the law shall pass away until all things have been accomplished? For the Christian who still awaits that End, there are very real problems concerning the law and its interpretation in Christ's injunction, "Whosoeuer therefore shal breake one of these least commandements, & teache men so, he shalbe called least in the kingdome of heauen" (Matt. 5 : 19).

St. Paul's "Love is the fulfilling of the law" sweeps away all legalistic difficulties—until one comes down to particular cases. In this matter of the relationship of Old Testament law to Christianity's New Dispensation—a relationship which eventually bears also on the relationship of real Jews to real Christians—the case of Henry VIII is particularly instructive. Cecil Roth, in his *History of the Jews in England,* writes that the King's "matrimonial difficulties . . . had a theological as well as a political aspect":

> For his desire to annul his long-standing marriage there was biblical authority in Leviticus xviii.16, in

> which an alliance between a man and his brother's wife is categorically forbidden. On the other hand, in Deuteronomy xxv.5, such a union is expressly prescribed if the brother had died childless, in order that his name should be perpetuated. The problem of interpretation was highly perplexing. In consequence the importance of Hebrew tradition for the correct comprehension of Holy Writ was suddenly realized. Since Jews were now excluded from both England and Spain, it was to the Jewish quarters of Italy, and especially to that of Venice, that both sides turned for guidance.[1]

Henry's emissaries found virtually the whole of the Venetian rabbinate hostile to his claims. "Worst of all," Cecil Roth writes, "at this very period a levirate marriage took place in Bologna between a Jew and his brother's widow. This completely discredited all arguments on the other side, and the breach between England and Rome was brought nearer" (145–46). Out of such legalistic niceties, in part at least, was the Protestant Reformation born.

What has St. Paul to do with Shakespeare? Or, for that matter, what has the levirate marriage of a Bolognese Jew got to do with *The Merchant of Venice?* Unless it was purely fortuitous, or a matter only of theatrical opportunism, that Shakespeare chose to write a play about the relation of Christians to Jews, and to emphasize also the relation of mercy to law, I think the answer must be, a great deal. I say that Shakespeare *chose* to write the play, because it was in fact an extraordinary choice to make. According to one scholar, there are extant, for the period from 1584 to 1627, only nine plays (including *The Merchant of Venice*) that contain anything like a recognizably Jewish character. Even if we add to this number references to three other

1. Cecil Roth, *A History of the Jews in England* (Oxford, 1941; 3rd ed. rev., 1964), p. 145.

plays, now lost, which may have contained a Jewish character, the subject matter remains unusual.[2] And of this handful of plays, only Marlowe's *The Jew of Malta* can seriously be compared with Shakespeare's play; not only are the others artistically inferior, but in each the Jewish character is only incidental to the action. The argument has occasionally been made that Shakespeare wrote *The Merchant of Venice* in response to the successful revival of *The Jew of Malta,* a success which is in turn attributed to the notorious case of Dr. Lopez, a Portuguese Jew who became Queen Elizabeth's physician and was hanged as a traitor in 1594. But none of this—the Lopez case nor *The Jew of Malta*—can "explain" *The Merchant of Venice,* any more than (for instance) later in Shakespeare's career the emerging popularity of Beaumont and Fletcher can "explain" the last romances.[3]

Even when all the nondramatic sources which have been claimed for *The Merchant of Venice* are taken into account, Shakespeare's decision to write about Christians and Jews remains remarkable. The simple point is worth making because some writers, trying either to accuse or acquit Shakespeare of anti-Semitism, imply that Shakespeare's subject matter was somehow culturally predetermined. Leslie Fiedler, for instance, assimilating the play into the archetypal theme of "the ogre and his daughter," finds it "small wonder . . . that everywhere in the popular Christian literature of Shakespeare's day—in the *Gesta Romanorum, Il Pecorone* of Ser Giovanni Fiorentino, Anthony Munday's *Zelauto,* the ballad of *Gernutus, The Jew of Venice,* even in Alexander Sylvaynes' *Orator* (presumably

2. The figures are those of J. L. Cardozo, *The Contemporary Jew in the Elizabethan Drama* (Paris, 1925; rpt. New York, 1955), p. 67.

3. An indispensable article on *The Jew of Malta* also contains material pertinent to *MV:* G. K. Hunter, "The Theology of *The Jew of Malta,*" *Journal of the Warburg and Courtauld Institutes,* 17 (1964): 211–40. Also see Alan C. Dessen, "The Elizabethan Stage Jew and Christian Example," *MLQ,* 35 (1974): 231–45.

a collection of moral debates rather than of fiction)—the mythic theme recurs, and that all these books not written originally in English were translated to feed the hunger which Shakespeare's and Marlowe's Jewish plays, as well as Gosson's lost *The Jew,* tried to appease."[4] But Fiedler's list, far from being selective, includes *all* the sources which can plausibly be claimed for Shakespeare's play; and in fact the only really indubitable source, *Il Pecorone,* was probably *not* translated into English. The evidence hardly points to any great Elizabethan hunger for Jewish plays, certainly not enough to make us attribute Shakespeare's choice to overwhelming popular demand.

Topical considerations such as the Lopez case or theatrical conditions cannot explain Shakespeare's decision to create a Shylock, and to set him in a court of law to argue his case against his Christian neighbors. Hence St. Paul and the politics of theology: specifically Christian considerations of serious Christian issues must, in part at least, have contributed to Shakespeare's extraordinary choice of subject matter, and influenced the dramatic embodiment of it. It is sometimes asked whether Shakespeare could have been personally acquainted with any Jews; it is a question of intrinsic interest, but little more relevant to the matter of Shakespeare's artistic intentions than whether (to take somewhat comparable cases) he could have known any introspective Danish princes or irascible old kings of ancient Britain. What Shakespeare certainly did know was his own culture's religious tradition, and his interest in the Jew he called Shylock must largely be attributed to that simple fact.

From an informed Christian perspective, Shakespeare saw that the relationships between the Old Testament and the New Testament, and between the Old Law and the New Law, are dynamic and problematic. As an artist, he saw various dramatic possibilities latent in those relation-

4. Fiedler, *Stranger in Shakespeare,* p. 124.

ships. He derived much of the material that shaped his fable from secular sources. Most importantly, he found in the novella *Il Pecorone* the basic ideas of the quest for a mysterious Lady of Belmonte, the flesh-bond that makes the quest possible, and the deadly threat of a usurious Jew. There, too, he found the prohibition against shedding blood in the exaction of the forfeiture. But the novella in no way supplied Shakespeare with a Shylock: of all the cardboard characters in *Il Pecorone,* the Jew is the least developed, and his religion is the merest fictional formality. Nor did the novella supply him with any suggestion for Portia's speech on "the quality of mercy," the speech which makes inescapably clear the element of Christian parable with which Shakespeare invested the story.

Portia's discourse on "The quality of mercy" (4.1.180–201) arises in a context which seems, at first glance, to make of it one of the most eloquent non sequiturs in English literature. Disguised as the "young and learned doctor" (4.1.144), Balthazar, Portia appears before the court and quickly establishes the facts. The identity of the litigants is sorted out with Portia's question, as significantly pointed as it is funny, "Which is the merchant here? and which the Jew?" (170). The prima facie soundness of Shylock's claim is affirmed:

> Of a strange nature is the suit you follow,
> Yet in such rule, that the Venetian law
> Cannot impugn you as you do proceed.
>
> [173–75]

And Antonio confesses the bond.

At this moment of utter impasse Portia lightly suggests her reasonable solution: "Then must the Jew be merciful" (178). There is sharp dramatic irony, both in the almost offhand remark—everything we know about Shylock, but which the supposed Balthazar can pretend not to know, tells us that Shylock will not be so lightly disposed to the reasonable suggestion—and also in the entire exchange it initiates. Portia's suggestion that the Jew "must . . . be merciful" affords Shylock a perfect opportunity to catch this Christian *au pied de la lettre*—a trick at which he has shown himself particularly adept in his first scene with Bassanio and Antonio. Quickly wrenching Portia's "must" out of her realm of easy sociability into his own harsh realm of legalism, Shylock demands to know, "On what compulsion *must* I, tell me that" (179). And Portia, feigning surprise but totally in control of the situation—a situation, it now appears, she has engineered to show that she too can be a master of literalism—as if more to gloss Shylock's "must" than anything else, offers to resolve the apparently minor verbal contretemps with her response, "The quality of mercy is not strain'd."

But far from constituting an attack on Shylock's position, the speech has, in context, the force of affirming it. Portia, herself for the nonce the representative of that law upon which Shylock stands, agrees (but as if never before having entertained so outlandish a suggestion) that indeed mercy cannot be constrained. And she concludes her moving but apparently irrelevant panegyric on mercy by dismissing it:

> I have spoke thus much
> To mitigate the justice of thy plea,
> Which if thou follow, this strict court of Venice
> Must needs give sentence 'gainst the merchant there.
> [4.1.198–201]

The original dilemma is in no way resolved by her speech; if anything it is made harsher, because more sharply defined, than before. After her speech there still stands, on the one side, the law Shylock craves, unmoveable, immutable, which Portia (despite Bassanio's urging) will not wrest to her authority: "It must not be, there is no power in Venice / Can alter a decree established" (214–15). And on the other side, apparently incapable of being brought into contact with its just opposite, stands mercy, the God-like attribute, which we pray for but cannot constrain.

So Portia, balked by Shylock in her appeal to mercy, must return to the law. And it is only after she has gone the full route of the law that we can properly understand her speech on mercy. That speech, then, is not an irrelevant setpiece. After she has completed her juridically curious performance as "Balthazar," which reveals the spirit of the law latent in its letter, yielding mercy through rigor, Portia's "mercy" can be seen in its full and proper relationship to its apparent opposite, the law.[5]

What Shakespeare, through Portia, does to the concept of law in *The Merchant of Venice* is similar to what Aeschylus, in the prototypical forensic comedy, does to the Erinyes: the law is tamed, civilized, put under the aegis of the Eumenides. In both *The Merchant of Venice* and *The Eumenides* the claims of the old law—its great age is especially emphasized by Aeschylus—cannot be denied, but they must be supplemented in such a way that this otherwise inflexible law is put into a more proper relationship to individual men, to society as a whole, and to divinity. Shylock's arguments for a strict construction are similar to the Erinyes': both stress the danger to society if the law is not fully honored; and the solution in both cases is similar: not an abrogration but a more comprehensive understanding of the nature of law, leading to its fulfillment both in justice and in mercy.

The principal model for Portia's procedure, with its revelation of a law that satisfies both justice and mercy, is to

5. D. J. Palmer, "Importance," nicely describes a part of the situation, but mistakes the conclusion: "[Portia's] eloquent appeal for mercy is probably the best known speech in the play, a set oration of great legal, moral, and passionate force. But the dramatic point of this speech seems to be its virtual irrelevance; it is a piece of superfluous rhetoric, since it achieves no effect whatsoever" (p. 114).

be found—whatever other literary analogues may be adduced—in no more arcane a source than the Gospel of St. Matthew. Indeed the Sermon on the Mount is, in its essential form, paradoxical in a way similar to Portia's argument in *The Merchant of Venice.* Its lesson is charity and mercy, but much of its context is severely legalistic. Christ makes the law stricter than it had ever been, but simultaneously more spiritual and inward:

> Ye haue heard that it was said vnto them of the olde time, Thou shalt not kil: for whosoeuer killeth, shal be culpable of iudgement. / But I say vnto you, whosoeuer is angrie with his brother vnaduisedly, shal be culpable of iudgment. . . .
>
> Ye haue heard that it hathe bene said, An eye for an eye, & a tooth for a tooth. / But I say vnto you, Resist not euil: but whoseuer shal smite thee on thy right cheke, turne to him the other also. [Matt. 5 : 21–22, 38–39]

It is such a law, with its equal regard for the letter and the spirit, that Christ comes not to overthrow but to fulfill.

The perfect fulfilling of the law, with its issue in mercy, is an ideal that goes beyond ordinary human possibilities into the realm of divine paradox. St. Augustine lucidly explicates part of that paradox. In his *Commentary on the Lord's Sermon on the Mount,* Augustine writes, concerning the text, "Till heaven and earth pass, one jot or one tittle shall in no wise pass from the law, till all be fulfilled" (Matt: 5 : 18), that it is "a vehement expression of perfection." But in one of the *Retractions* added to the original commentary, Augustine asks "whether this perfection can be understood in such a way that it is nevertheless true to say that in this life no one lives without sin while using free will":

> Could the Law be fulfilled even to the last tittle, except, indeed, by a man who observes all the divine commandments? As a matter of fact in those commandments we are bidden to say: "Forgive us our sins, even as we forgive those who sin against us," and to the end of the world the whole Church is saying that prayer. Therefore, all the commandments are accounted as fulfilled when forgiveness is granted for whatever is not fulfilled.[6]

According to Augustine's original commentary, Christ, in saying that he comes to fulfill the Law, "says either that He is going to make it complete by adding what it lacks or that He is going to observe it by doing what it contains" (11 : 37). The Retraction makes clear that the essential thing added to the law by Christ is forgiveness. Mercy, therefore, is made part of the law, rather than an opposing principle. Indeed mercy, or forgiveness, becomes the legal principle enabling all other legal principles; we are commanded to pray for forgiveness and to forgive others, and only when both parts of that commandment have been fulfilled can all the rest of the law be accounted as fulfilled.

It is impossible for fallen man, exercising his free will, to be perfect in the law except through the gift of mercy; only the unmerited forgiveness of his sins, not his own sinful nature, can accomplish the Christ-like fulfillment. This of course is a line of thought which had particular appeal to Protestant theologians; and in the homily "Of Salvation" (one of the *Certain Sermons Appointed by the Queen's Majesty . . . For the Better Understanding of the Simple People,* 1547—a text, probably by Cranmer, any Elizabethan would have had difficulty escaping) the thought is developed in a manner particularly relevant to *The Mer-*

6. St. Augustine, *Commentary on the Lord's Sermon on the Mount,* trans. Denis J. Kavanagh, in *The Fathers of the Church* (New York, 1951), 11 : 203.

chant of Venice. The homily ringingly asserts the central Protestant doctrine of justification by faith alone:

> For all the good works that we can do be imperfect, and therefore not able to deserve our justification: But our justification doth come freely by the mere mercy of God, and of so great and free mercy, that whereas all the World was not able of themselves to pay any part towards their ransom, it pleased our heavenly Father, of his infinite mercy, without any our desert or deserving, to prepare for us the most precious Jewels of Christ's body and blood, whereby our ransom might be fully paid, the Law fulfilled, and his Justice fully satisfied. So that Christ is now the righteousness of all them that truly do believe in him. He for them paid their ransom by his death. He for them fulfilled the Law in his life. So that now *in him, and by him every true Christian man may be called a fulfiller of the law,* forasmuch as that which their infirmity lacked, Christ's Justice hath supplied.

Portia, as the young lawyer drawing out every jot and tittle of law until it reveals its end in mercy, is therefore doing nothing which is not possible for anyone—but only in and by Christ:

> Therefore Jew,
> Though justice be thy plea, consider this,
> That in the course of justice, none of us
> Should see salvation: we do pray for mercy,
> And that same prayer doth teach us all to render
> The deeds of mercy.
>
> [4.1.193–98]

"That same prayer" is, of course, the Lord's Prayer. And here, with a delicate play on words, Portia suggests how that prayer makes an apparently inflexible law yield the unconstrainable gift: to perform the act of mutual forgiveness becomes, in her quasi-legalistic phrase, "to *render* / The *deeds* of mercy." The careful juxtaposition of "deeds" and "mercy" points toward the essence of this Christian comedy.

The relationship of mercy and justice had been a favorite subject among Christian writers long before Shakespeare, because of its centrality to their faith, but also because of its innately dramatic possibilities. The subject had been especially popular in a form known as the Parliament of Heaven or the Four Daughters of God; in this form it was widespread throughout medieval Europe, and is extant in English in *Piers Plowman,* the N-Town (or *Ludus Coventriae*) play of *The Salutation and Conception,* and in the morality *Castle of Perseverance.* The allegory is essentially an elaboration of a single verse, the tenth, of Psalm 85: "Mercie and Trueth shal mete: righteousnes and peace shal kisse one another." Several critics who perceive an element of Christian allegory in *The Merchant of Venice* have suggested the relevance of the Four Daughters' debate to the situation in Shakespeare's comedy. It is worth pausing over briefly.[7]

In European Books of Hours from the fifteenth and sixteenth centuries the allegory of the Four Daughters is "generally associated with the Annunciation" (Chew, p. 62), as it is in the play from the English N-Town cycle. That anonymous play seems to me the most intelligent and dramatically satisfying treatment of the theme in English, setting aside our own problematic case of *The Merchant of Venice,* and can serve as our exemplar. In it, God the Father hears his creatures' anguished cries for mercy, and responds:

7. The fullest account of the allegorical tradition is in Hope Traver, *The Four Daughters of God* (Bryn Mawr, 1907). See also Gollancz, *Allegory and Mysticism;* Samuel C. Chew, *The Virtues Reconciled: An Iconographic Study* (Toronto, 1947); Coghill, "Basis of Shakespearian Comedy"; Honor Matthews, *Character and Symbol in Shakespeare's Plays* (Cambridge, 1962).

Now xal I ryse that am Almyghty,
Time is come of reconsyliacion,
My prophetys with prayers have made supplicacion,
My contryte creaturys crye alle for comforte.[8]

But Truth, the first of the four daughters to speak, objects to the proposed "reconsyliacion," reminding the Father of the law that "Twey contraryes mow not togedyr dwell": since God has condemned Adam to death and hell, to restore him to bliss would violate God's inviolable word. Now, after Mercy has pleaded on Mankind's behalf and Justice has seconded Truth's position, the conflict between the equally fundamental but incompatible principles of reconciliation and of contrariety is further complicated when Peace has her say. Peace finds that Truth and Justice "say grett reson," but she inclines to her sister Mercy:

ffor yf mannys sowle xulde abyde in helle,
Betwen God and man evyr xulde be dyvysyon,
And then myght not I Pes dwelle.

On all sides, then, the central ideal of unity is stressed, but precisely therein lies the impasse: since two contraries may not go together, God cannot now deny the justice of his sentence against mankind; but unless that justice is somehow altered there will remain the intolerable division "betwen God and man."

This is the substance of the Four Daughters' debate. Now, unable by themselves to resolve the dilemma, they agree to Peace's suggestion to let God himself arbitrate. (Justice's words here are especially interesting: she is content to put the matter to God "ffor in hym is very equyte." The distinction is between her own legalistic "Justicia" or "Ryghtwysness" and a more comprehensive "equity" which belongs to God.) It is decided that a sacrifice must be found to un-

8. Quoted from the edition of *Ludus Coventriae* by James O. Halliwell (London, 1841), unlineated.

dergo and fulfill God's justice; the members of the Trinity go into council, and the Son concludes:

ffadyr, he that xal do this must be bothe God and man,
    Lete me se how I may were that wede,
And sythe in my wysdam he began
    I am redy to do this dede.

The Holy Spirit makes a magnificent conclusion to the debate portion of the play, stressing again the importance of unity, but now also of love, the principle that can satisfy both the law of contrariety and of reconciliation:

I the Holy Gost of yow tweyn do procede,
    This charge I wole take on me,
I love to your lover xal yow lede,
    This is the assent of oure unyte.

Mercy speaks the verse from Psalm 85, God's four daughters kiss, and Gabriel is sent to Mary with his message of peace.

The Merchant of Venice is not a mystery play nor a morality play nor even, in any moderately strict use of the word, consistently an allegory. But it has a significance that can be generalized beyond the immediate story; and part of that more general significance is the problem, in a specifically Christian context, of reconciling justice and mercy. Sir Israel Gollancz was too diffident in the way he offered the allegory of the Four Daughters as an analogue to *The Merchant of Venice:* "I do not wish for a moment to suggest that anything of this was in Shakespeare's mind, but the drama of allegory was by no means dead in Shakespeare's time, and the medieval art of exposition by means of *exempla* was very near in kinship to actual allegory." [9] The parabolic intention of the play did not seep into it by cultural osmosis; it is a product of Shakespeare's conscious art. And lest we miss it, Shakespeare has Portia explicitly

9. Gollancz, *Allegory and Mysticism,* p. 40.

direct us to find a universal applicability in the drama: "in the course of justice, *none of us* / Should see salvation."

In calling attention to elements of allegory or parable in the play—and they are not discrete, but inform the structure of the whole—I am aware of the dangers of reductionism. The formula, "Portia is actually Mercy personified" (Gollancz, p. 27), is wrong insofar as it is too limiting. Frequently Portia is the personification of nothing other than the Shakespearean romantic heroine, and is all the more interesting for the fact. It is Portia, not Misericordia, who describes her suitors for Nerissa's delight, or who plays upon the humorous possibilities of her disguise:

> I'll prove the prettier fellow of the two,
> And wear my dagger with the braver grace,
> And speak between the change of man and boy,
> With a reed voice, and turn two mincing steps
> Into a manly stride. . . .
>
> [3.4.64–68]

But in Shakespeare's defiantly "impure" art, a parable may be complicated without being confused. It is complicated by a degree of psychological and circumstantial elaboration alien to an older didactic drama. And it is complicated too by the greater thoroughness with which Shakespeare explores the latencies in even the most apparently simple of ideas.

In heaven, the rival claims of justice and mercy, or (to translate the debate into the terms of Reformation polemics) those of the works of law versus the free gift of grace, are harmoniously resolved. But on earth, among mere mortals, the dynamic, dialectical nature of the debate has insured its continuance from the earliest days of the Church. The secular dimension of the debate—its applicability, that is, to the realm of purely human law—is just as acute as the theological. For jurist as well as theologian, for believer and nonbeliever alike, the contest between equally fundamental but apparently divergent tendencies—toward the external compulsion of law, on the one hand, and the internal movement toward freedom from constraint, on the other—never ceases.[10] In Scripture, that enduring tension is suggested by two of the statements we have already encountered here: Paul's "by faith without the workes of the Law," and Matthew's "one iote, or one title of the Law shal not scape."

There is no way to prove that Shakespeare had the Epistle to the Romans in mind, as well as the primary material of the Sermon on the Mount, when he composed *The Merchant of Venice;* but I find it highly likely that he did. Even the rhetoric of that Epistle, with its frequent question-and-answer technique, its extraordinary degree of formal elaboration, and its careful—if at times bewildering—logical development, is a rhetoric especially congenial to the Elizabethan habit of mind. Shakespeare was a master of a similar rhetorical form—a form, interestingly, which he uses most frequently in his comedies, and there most often to satirize abuses of rhetoric and logic. One might compare, for instance, Paul's worrying the logic of sin and grace, and of mankind's fortunate fall into an era of law—

> Moreouer the Law entred thereupon that the offence shulde abunde: neuertheles where sinne abunded, there grace abunded muche more. . . . What shal we say then? Shal we continue stil in sinne, that grace may abunde? God forbid— [Rom. 5 : 20, 6 : 1–2]

with some of the more astonishing flights of Shakespearean comic rhetoric. The logic which almost leads Paul to the conclusion ("God forbid") that there is an obligation to sin so "that grace may abound" has affinities with the logic

10. For a legal scholar's interesting perspective on these issues, see Harold J. Berman, *The Interaction of Law and Religion* (Nashville, 1974).

Berowne uses, in *Love's Labor's Lost,* to provide a mock-Pauline "salve for perjury" for "affection's men-at-arms" (*LLL,* 4.3.285–86):

> [Let] us once lose our oaths to find ourselves,
> Or else we lose ourselves to keep our oaths.
> It is religion to be thus forsworn:
> For charity itself fulfills the law,
> And who can sever love from charity?
>
> [4.3.358–62]

One might think also of Falstaff's catechism on honor or, still more pertinently, Launcelot Gobbo deciding the rival claims of his hard conscience and the friendly fiend (2.2.1–30).

Parody of the sacred would not have been as obscure or as shocking to an Elizabethan as it is to us. Shakespeare's audience, still spiritually and esthetically akin to the audience for whom the Wakefield Master wrote *The Second Shepherds' Play,* could be counted on to see the serious implications (which in no way nullify the comic effect) of such parody; in Berowne's speech, for instance, they would immediately have seen the way in which St. Paul's text is being wrenched from its spiritual context into the most outrageously carnal—and comic—sphere. And when they heard and saw the strange comic business in which Launcelot decides to leave "a rich Jew's service, to become / The servant of so poor a gentleman" as the Christian Bassanio (2.2.140–41), the entire interlude might have seemed a preposterous redaction of Christ's injunction in the Sermon on the Mount, "No man can serue two masters: for either he shal hate the one, and loue the other, or els he shal leane to the one, and despise the other. Ye can not serue God and riches" (Matt. 6 : 24). In Launcelot's debate, his conscience, "hanging about the neck of [his] heart," counsels loyalty to the Jew his master, "who (God bless the mark) is a kind of devil"; while "the fiend, who (saving your reverence) is the devil himself," urges Launcelot to run away.

It would be a mistake to accept Launcelot's "confusions" as our own conclusions; his summary statement that "Certainly the Jew is the very devil incarnation" just will not do (even in translation) as an adequate commentary on Shylock. Launcelot's decision to put his heels at the fiend's commandment, "because the fiend gives the more friendly counsel," is surely a case of the right deed for the wrong reason; but it may serve to remind an audience of Paul's words to the Gentiles concerning their new freedom, under grace, from the law.

> What then? shal we sinne, because we are not vnder the Law, but vnder grace? God forbid. / Know ye not, that to whomesoeuer ye giue your selues as seruants to obey, his seruants ye are to whome ye obey, whether it be of sinne vnto death, or of obedience vnto righteousnes? / But God be thanked, that ye haue bene the seruants of sinne, but ye haue obeyed from the heart vnto the forme of the doctrine, wherevnto ye were deliuered. / Being then made fre from sinne, ye are made the seruants of righteousnes. [Rom. 6 : 15–18]

Other aspects of the Gobbo family's business in 2.2 seem also to be informed with ironic reflections of Scripture. Old Gobbo enters, seeking "the way to Master Jew's" where his son dwells:

> O heavens! [Launcelot says, aside] this is my true-begotten father, who being more than sand-blind, high gravel-blind, knows me not—I will try confusions with him. [33–35]

The old man's blindness, and Launcelot's ensuing confusions of him, may remind us of a famous deception practiced on an earlier patriarch: "And when Izhak was olde,

& his eies were dimme (so that he colde not se) he called Esau his eldest sonne, and said vnto him, My sonne" (Gen. 27 : 1). The likelihood that Shakespeare intends an allusion to the story of Jacob and Esau here is increased by Jacob's indubitable presence at other places in the play. Shylock has already been heard (1.3.66 ff.) debating the question of usury, and adducing in its support the time "when Jacob graz'd his uncle Laban's sheep." Shylock makes his oath "by Jacob's staff" (2.5.36), and his wife's name, like that of Jacob's first wife, was Leah.[11]

According to the biblical account, Esau had in effect been disinherited before birth, although he was the older son and therefore by law should have been the inheritor of his father's blessing: "And the Lord said to [Rebecca], two nations are in thy wombe, and two maner of people shalbe deuided out of thy bowels, and the one people shalbe mightier then the other, and the elder shal serue the yonger" (Gen. 25 : 23). This extraordinary precedence, given by special dispensation to the younger son Jacob, may help explain Launcelot Gobbo's social pretensions. Launcelot insists upon being called "Master Launcelot," though Old Gobbo protests that he is "No 'master' sir, but a poor man's son" (2.2.48). There ensues that oddly *Lear*-like moment when Launcelot asks, "Do you not know me father?" and Old Gobbo replies, "Alack sir I am sand-blind, I know you not" (70–71). And now Launcelot, who to confuse his father had announced his own death, must try to convince the old man that he is indeed "Launcelot, your boy that was, your son that is, your child that shall be" (80–83)—while the suspicious father withholds his blessing.

In Genesis, when Rebecca plots to steal Isaac's blessing for her younger son, Jacob objects: "Beholde, Esau my

11. Brown, Arden ed., notes that "Henley (Var. '78) saw allusions to the deception practised on the blindness of Isaac; cf. the recognition by feeling Launcelot's hair" (p. 39). I owe the initial suggestion to a nearer source, Professor T. P. Roche, Jr. of Princeton University.

brother is rough, and I am smothe. / My father maie possibly fele me, and I shal seme to him to be a mocker" (27 : 11–12). Therefore Rebecca covers Jacob's hands and neck with goats' skins; and the old man, touching what he thinks are the hands of Esau, gives his blessing. Smooth indeed! The most pious exegete may be permitted to see potential moral difficulties, and therefore perhaps the possibility for comedy, in this episode. Sixteenth-century commentators seem unsure what to make of it. After all, Rebecca had received God's word that Esau, the elder, would serve the younger: why, then, this anxiety to hasten along God's work? The commentator in the Geneva Bible concludes that "This subtiltie is blameworthie because [Rebecca] shulde haue taried til God had performed his promes," and that "Althogh Iaakob was assured of this blessing by faith: yēt he did euil to seke it by lies and the more because he abuseth Gods Name thereunto." Martin Luther, however, after acknowledging that it is "a very weighty question and an almost unsolvable problem," exonerates mother and son: "That which has been given to me by God and concerning which I know that it belongs to me I can claim by using any deception and scheme; for at the risk of committing a mortal sin I am bound to plan, invent, pretend, and conceal in order that what has been committed to me by God may come to pass." [12] However one decides the moral issue, the episode is sufficiently memorable for it to inform the action between Gobbo father and son, as Old Gobbo, blindly reaching out and touching the back of the kneeling Launcelot's head, exclaims: "Lord worshipp'd might he be, what a beard hast thou got! Thou hast got more hair on thy chin, than Dobbin my fill-horse has on his tail" (2.2.89–91).

The comic business has its serious point, and the story of Jacob's blessing is pertinent to Shakespeare's concerns in

12. Martin Luther, *Lectures on Genesis,* in *Works,* ed. Jaroslav Pelikan (St. Louis, 1968), 5 : 113.

The Merchant of Venice. St. Paul, in Romans 9, gives his reading of the story of Jacob and Esau, which concerns (as the headnote in the Geneva Bible succinctly puts it) "the vocation of the Gentiles, And the reiection of the Iewes." Old Gobbo's blessing on his son's hairy head is thus a comic allusion to the Christian scheme of salvation-history. Esau (Paul suggests) is the type of the Jew, to whom the blessing would have belonged under the law, but who carelessly sold his spiritual patrimony for the sake of the flesh; Jacob is the type of the Christian, called under Grace, "that the purpose of God might remaine according to election, not by workes, but by him that calleth" (Rom. 9 : 11).

According to St. Paul, the spiritual man, freed from the flesh, is "deliuered from the Law, being dead vnto it" (Rom. 7 : 6). As Paul wrestles with the inevitable next stage of his argument—"What shal we say then? Is the Law sinne? God forbid" (7 : 7)—he reveals some of the complexities in the role of law under this new dispensation, and thereby takes us nearer to the question of law as it emerges in Shakespeare's Venetian courtroom. God's moral law cannot be sin; still, according to Paul, "I knewe not sinne, but by the Law: for I had not knowen lust, except the Law had said, Thou shalt not lust" (Rom. 7 : 7). It is sin that abuses the law, making of the commandments the occasions for concupiscence: "But sinne toke an occasion by the commandement, and disceived me, and thereby slew me. / Wherefore the Law is holie, and the commandement is holie, and iust, & good" (Rom. 7 : 11–12)—and an important function of this good law is to teach man the nature of sin:

> Was that then which is good, made death vnto me? God forbid: but sinne, that it might appeare sinne, wroght death in me by that which is good, that sinne might be out of measure sinful by the commandement. / For we knowe that the Law is spiritual, but I am carnal, sold vnder sin. [Rom. 7 : 13–14]

In making sin appear *as* sin, God's law performs the crucial didactic function that Portia will make Venice's law perform, making man aware of his inevitably sinful nature (since no man can perform all the works of the law), and hence of his dependence upon God for salvation.

Our first meeting with Portia in *The Merchant of Venice* introduces, however lightly, the problem of law versus spiritual freedom. "The will of a dead father" that Portia must obey is a "hard" decree; and Portia finds herself caught up in the war between the opposing laws of the spirit and of the flesh:

> If to do were as easy as to know what were good to do, chapels had been churches, and poor men's cottages princes' palaces,—it is a good divine that follows his own instructions,—I can easier teach twenty what were good to be done, than be one of the twenty to follow mine own teaching: the brain may devise laws for the blood, but a hot temper leaps o'er a cold decree. . . . [1.2.12–19]

Here at the very start Portia suggests her crucial role as a teacher whose first lesson is her own exemplary confession of ignorance and dependency (cf. 3.2.159–67). With her lightly recounted dilemma we might compare the powerful conclusion to Paul's crucial seventh chapter of Romans. There too we see what it means to know one law and follow another:

> I finde then by the Law, that when I wolde do good, euil is present with me. / For I delite in the Law of God, concerning the inward man: / But I se another law in my membres, rebelling against the lawe of my minde, & leading me captiue vnto the law of sinne, which is in my membres. / O wretched man that I am, who shal deliuer me from the bodie of this death? / I thanke God through Jesus Christ our Lord. Then I

> my self in my minde serue the Law of God, but in my flesh the law of sinne.

In *The Merchant of Venice,* where divine considerations are kept firmly in touch with the realities of mankind's fallen condition, this conflict of laws will not easily be cleared away. The harmonious resolution of a timeless dilemma will be accomplished only after a juridically—and dramatically—necessary period of time.

Beneath Shylock's Jewish gabardine some critics think they can discern the lineaments of an Elizabethan Puritan.[13] Besides several externally similar characteristics—sobriety and thrift, hypocrisy and separatism—they point to the Puritans' "rigid emphasis on the law" (Millward, p. 159). An early—and by far the funniest—recognition of this "judaizing" tendency in Puritanism is Ben Jonson's in *Bartholomew Fair:* there, the Puritan "Rabbi," Zeal-of-the-land Busy, argues that it will be lawful to eat pig, "so it be eaten with a reformed mouth," since it will "profess our hate and loathing of Judaism, whereof the brethren stand taxed" (1.6.45 ff.).

But extremes tend to meet, and it is at least as plausible to see Roman Catholic abuses reflected in Shylock. The man who cries, "My deeds upon my head! I crave the law" (4.1.202), is arrogantly presuming on the efficacy of his works in a way that, according to English Protestant polemics, the Catholics did "in Dormitory, in Cloyster, in Chapter, in choice of meats and drinks, and in such like things." [14]

The equation of Roman Catholicism with Judaism was as much a commonplace (especially in antimonastic polemics) as the equation of Puritanism with Judaism. The Catholics,

13. E.g., Kirschbaum, *Character and Characterization;* Paul N. Seigel, *Shakespeare in His Time and Ours;* Peter Millward, *Shakespeare's Religious Background* (London, 1973); J. Leeds Barroll, *Artificial Persons* (Columbia, S.C., 1974).

14. *Certain Sermons* (1574), the homily "Of Good Works."

indeed, were said to be even worse than the Jews in their blind reliance on empty works, mere external forms and ceremonies, as if God's grace could somehow be bought in mankind's shoddy marts. The English homilist, after criticising the ancient Scribes and Pharisees, draws the parallel between the Jews of the old dispensation and his own days' papists:

> Neither had the *Jews* in their most blindness so many pilgrimages unto images, nor used so much kneeling, kissing, and censing of them, as hath been used in our time. Sects and feigned Religions were neither the fortieth part so many among the Jews, nor more superstitiously and ungodlily abused, than of late days they have been among us. Which Sects and Religions had so many hypocritical and feigned works in their state of Religion (as they arrogantly named it) that their lamps (as they said) ran always over, able to satisfy, not only their own sins, but also for all other their benefactors, brothers and sisters of Religion, as most ungodlily and craftily they had persuaded the multitude of ignorant people.[15]

As his answer to the Catholics' supposed reliance on the works of the law, the English reformer boldly declares the doctrine of justification by faith alone—"the strong rock and foundation of the Christian religion":

> Consider diligently these words, without Works by Faith only, freely we receive remission of our sins. What can be spoken more plainly, than to say, That freely without Works, by Faith only, we obtain remission of our sins? [16]

Indeed what can be spoken more plainly?—except that the ringing assertion is immediately followed by an acknowledgment and warning, that "carnal men" may misunder-

15. Ibid.
16. *Certain Sermons* (1574), homily "Of Salvation."

stand the doctrine and "take unjustly occasion thereby to live carnally, after the appetite and will of the world, the flesh, and the devil." And repeatedly, in the homilies "Of Salvation," "Of Good Works," "Of Faith," and "Of Alms Deeds," the Protestant writer asserts the unique efficacy of faith only to append, in horror, a warning against the antinomianism which "carnal men" may read into his central doctrine.

Thus, in their churches and elsewhere, the men of Shakespeare's age heard repeatedly the potential for conflict in the apparently irreconcilable tendencies toward grace or toward law, faith or works. How to preserve the place of good works and obedience to law while maintaining the doctrine of justification by faith alone? The homily "Of Salvation" makes clear that the weighing of merits and demerits, reward and punishment, cannot lead to a proper understanding. The primacy of faith must be maintained; and the reformers therefore insist that good works *follow* faith, that they are inevitably the fruits of faith.

The English Church's careful balance is reflected in its Thirty-nine Articles. The eleventh, "Of the Justification of Man," asserts uncompromisingly that "We are accounted righteous before God, only for the merit of our Lord and Saviour Jesus Christ by faith, and not for our own works, or deservings." But the twelfth, "Of Good Works" (one of four articles added by Archbishop Parker to an earlier version),[17] draws upon the familiar metaphor of "the fruits of faith":

> Albeit that good works, which are the fruits of faith, and follow after Justification, cannot put away our sins, and endure the severity of God's judgment, yet are they pleasing and acceptable to God in Christ, and do spring out necessarily of a true and lively faith, insomuch that by them a lively faith may be as evidently known, as a tree discerned by the fruit.

17. Horton Davies, *Worship and Theology in England: From Cranmer to Hooker 1534–1603* (Princeton, 1970), p. 23.

The horticultural metaphor, derived from Scripture, is ubiquitous:[18] "a dead faith" is one "which bringeth forth no good works, but is idle, barren, and unfruitful"; but the true faith "is lively and fruitful in bringing forth good works" ("Of Faith"). The homily "Of Salvation," which has roundly declared the inefficacy of works, concludes by invoking the metaphor: "These be the fruits of true faith: to do good as much as lieth in us to every man; and, above all things, and in all things, to advance the glory of God of whom only we have our sanctification, justification, salvation, and redemption."

Though Portia has no need for the technical terms, this is very much like the lesson she teaches, through her juridical demonstration in the Venetian courtroom. Obedience to law—even that curious one on which Shylock stands so falsely secure—although a necessity, cannot be imputed as a merit to us. Shylock's is a law of death, the killing law of the letter. *Lively* works of law can grow only out of the faith that convinces us of God's absolute power and justice, of our weakness and insufficiency, and thus of our need to glorify—precisely through observance of the charitable works of a lively law—God's mercy.

18. Among its scriptural sources are: Matt. 7 : 18–20, John 15, Romans 6 : 21–22, James 3 : 26.

3

"This Strict Court of Venice" Law and Language, Miracle and Myth in *The Merchant of Venice*

It is a pedagogical truism that all drama involves conflict. Any dramatic resolution therefore implies some judgment on the issues in the conflict. But when a court of law stands at the center of the drama, certain peculiarities may result. The abstract, theoretical issues behind the fiction's particular conflict may become more prominent than in other drama—especially if, as in *The Merchant of Venice,* the bare facts of the case are not in dispute. Thus forensic drama may be a curious and often a disturbing combination of the minutely and realistically particular—the legal intricacies, that is, of *this* case—and of the universal. Such drama easily tends toward the didactic and allegorical, for in any court of law the individual is judged according to standards that pertain to all: in a sense, the One inevitably stands for the Many, as in the archetypal Christian forensic drama where the Parliament of Heaven argues Mankind's fate and one single Man undergoes the penalty. And the mechanics of the court itself may come under scrutiny, as it does, for instance, in *Volpone* and *The White Devil, The Eumenides* and *The Merchant of Venice.* In such plays we are asked to judge not only the resolution of the particular issues in the conflict, but the means by which that resolution is achieved and the standards implied by those means. Forensic drama tends to be a self-conscious drama, allowing us, through the metaphor of the courtroom, to glimpse its own judgmental principles.

One may therefore applaud the following typical trumpet blast by E. E. Stoll: "The juristic disquisitions of the Germans on the issue [of legal procedure] in *The Merchant of Venice* are among the most misguided and wasted of human exertions," without, however, agreeing with the statement it amplifies: "Law in Shakespeare is, save for phrases and incidental matters or what is taken out of the novel or chronicle he is dramatizing, nothing but stage law." [1] The dismissive "nothing but" short-circuits the real question. Historical research into the laws of contemporary England or Venice may indeed yield little of value; but the nature of Shakespeare's "stage law" is not something to be taken for granted.[2] Precisely because this "stage law" cannot be found codified in the statutes of any realm it is of special interest to us; and at those points where Shakespeare's stage courtroom fails to correspond to what we know of the procedures of any other courtroom we must ask why Shakespeare, especially in that notoriously litigious time, has wrested his fiction away from historical verisimilitude.

It is essential for Shakespeare's purposes in this play that Venetian law should seem to bear no signs of the concept of equity; it must be the unmitigated law of the letter, so that "this strict court of Venice" must indeed "give sentence 'gainst the merchant there" (4.1.200–201) if he has incurred "the penalty and forfeit" spelled out in the least letter of the bond. Of course Shakespeare was aware of the anomalies in these stage proceedings. Among other things, he was aware of the development in England, during the preceding two centuries, of the Court of Chancery, a court guided by

1. E. E. Stoll, *Shakespeare Studies* (New York, 1927; rpt. 1942), p. 71.

2. Two recent, respectable studies of Shakespeare's knowledge of civil law are: O. Hood Phillips, *Shakespeare and the Lawyers* (London, 1972), which has a good account of past scholarship and pseudoscholarship; W. Nicholas Knight, *Shakespeare's Hidden Life* (New York, 1973).

the concept of equity rather than of strict legalism. The Chancellor's court was "a court of conscience appointed to mitigate the rigor of proceeding at law." [3] It was less bound by precedent than the court of common law, and it operated with less procedural formality, allowing it (in theory at least) leeway to dispense *moral* justice—the spirit of the law—in cases where common law was constrained by the letter of procedure and precedent. F. W. Maitland gives the following account of the fourteenth-century beginnings of the Chancellor's court of conscience:

> Very often the petitioner [to the king] requires some relief at the expense of some other person. He complains that for some reason or another he cannot get a remedy in the ordinary court of justice and yet he is entitled to a remedy. He is poor, he is old, he is sick, his adversary is rich and powerful, will bribe or intimidate jurors, *or has by some trick or some accident acquired an advantage of which the ordinary courts with their formal procedure will not deprive him.* The petition is often couched in piteous terms, the king is asked to find a remedy *for the love of God and in the way of charity.* Such petitions are referred by the king to the Chancellor. Gradually in the course of the fourteenth-century petitioners, instead of going to the king, will go straight to the Chancellor, will address their complaints to him and adjure him to do what is right for the love of God and in the way of charity.[4]

During the Elizabethan period, common lawyers and the Chancellor became involved in jurisdictional disputes: it was a local, secular stage of the endless debate between Mercy and Justice.

3. S. P. D. Eliz. (Add.), p. 99, Nov. 5, 1583; quoted in Tawney's edition of Wilson's *Discourse upon Usury,* p. 13.

4. F. W. Maitland, *Equity,* ed. A. H. Chaytor and W. J. Whittaker (Cambridge, 1909), pp. 4–5, my italics.

Shakespeare had good reason to be aware of developments in the equity system.[5] His father had brought a suit at common law in 1589 (Shakespeare *v.* Lambert), over a dispute which dated from 1580. In 1597, still litigating this case, John Shakespeare instituted proceedings in the Chancellor's court; but (shades of *Bleak House!*) the matter never was resolved. John's son had better success in his own two appeals to the Court of Chancery: in 1611, along with other Stratfordians who, with the playwright, held the leases on certain tithes, he complained (using the form usual to Chancery) that he was "against all equity and good conscience" liable to unjustified and extraordinary expenses; and in 1615 he joined in a suit concerning some property in Blackfriars. In both suits Shakespeare obtained the relief he sought.[6]

So Shakespeare knew that even in 1596 or 1597 recourse from the unreasonable rigor of the common law was available in equity, despite all the system's inadequacies and despite the fact—which has special bearing on the situation in *The Merchant of Venice*—that "the equity of redemption had not yet been elevated into a general rule, and mortgages were therefore liable to total forfeiture to unscrupulous speculators." [7] The polarities established at the outset of the trial in *The Merchant of Venice*—on the one hand, Shylock's "I crave the law," and on the other, Bassanio's "Wrest once the law to your authority,— / To do a great right, do a little wrong" (4.1.202, 211–12)—are the polarities of a

5. See, in addition to the books mentioned in note 2 (above), Gordon W. Zeeveld, *The Temper of Shakespeare's Thought* (New Haven, 1964), pp. 141–59. An article that appeared too late for me to use in this account is by E. F. J. Tucker, "The Letter of the Law in *The Merchant of Venice*," *Shakespeare Survey*, 29 (1976): 93–101. Tucker is harsh on previous scholarship; he asserts that equity was a concept rooted in common law. Despite his aggrieved tone, his conclusions do little to alter one's sense of the place of equity *in the play*.

6. G. E. Bentley, *Shakespeare: A Biographical Handbook* (New Haven, 1961), pp. 46, 86.

7. Stone, *Crisis of the Aristocracy*, p. 539.

very special fictive situation, with a relationship to actual judicial practice (as an English audience would know it) made the more interesting by the obliquity.

Portia's response to Bassanio's plea that she wrest the law to her authority is uncompromising: "It must not be, there is no power in Venice / Can alter a decree established" (214–15). Such an unalterable law—a law that regards only the act with no regard to person, that knows no spirit apart from its letter—touches a deep fear in us. It is the fear of a diabolical literalism, and it is especially apprehended by dreamers and by such fabulists of the unconscious as Kafka, for instance, or Borges, or even the Brothers Grimm. It is the fear of being trapped by the word itself rather than by the intent of the word; and although lawyers may protest the comparison, it is a fear known also by litigants in court: the courtroom is archetypally an arena where bright logic and dark mystery mingle, where language, codified into law, assumes a virtual power of its own and becomes a potentially uncontrollable menace. In court our every word will be taken down; anything we say may be used in evidence against us. A quotidian echo of our fear of diabolical literalism is heard in the advice to "read the fine print": the lurking word, ready to spring its surprises on us, is felt to be dangerous whether the contract is tendered by a mortal merchant or (as often in fiction) by the arch-literalist, the devil himself.

The theme of the dangerous binding word is widespread, especially in popular forms of literature. In the folk tale of "The Three Wishes," the most ordinary sort of discourse becomes charged with comic perils when contact with a miraculous power vivifies ordinarily dead metaphors:

> A little man came to a wee house on a wet day and asked for supper, and they gave him a bowl of soup and some bread, and when he went he gave them a little round thing, and it would give him [*sic*] three

> wishes. So the next morning the man said, "Soup again! I wish I had a pudding for a change!" And there was a pudding. "Oh, you fool!" said the wife, "One wish is gone! I wish the pudding was on your head!" And it was. "That's two wishes gone!" said the man. The wife said, "You ought to have wished for a bar of gold or anything." "I wish the pudding was off my head," said the man. And that was the three wishes gone.[8]

Names are often the vehicles of diabolical literalism. In the tale "Nicht Nought Nothing," a confusion between the title's three words as common signifiers and as a proper name leads to a potentially ghastly outcome: A king has been long away from home, and in his absence his wife has given birth to a son; returning, the king finds his way blocked by a big river:

> But a giant came up to him and said, "If you will give me Nicht Nought Nothing, I will carry you over the water on my back." The king had never heard that his son was called Nicht Nought Nothing, and so he promised him. When the king got home again, he was very pleased to see his queen again, and his young son. She told him she had not given the child any name but Nicht Nought Nothing until he should come home himself. The poor king was in a terrible case. He said: "What have I done? I promised to give the giant who carried me over the river on his back Nicht Nought Nothing." [Briggs, Pt. A, I : 424]

After the most astonishing hairbreadth 'scapes the story has a happy ending; but for a time it looks as though diabolical literalism has converted a tripled negative into an everything.

The Grimms' "Rumpel-Stilts-Ken" also involves both the

8. Katherine M. Briggs, *A Dictionary of British Folk-Tales,* Pt. A: Folk Narratives (London, 1970), 1 : 522.

autonomously powerful name and the theme of the binding promise. The demanded forfeit in "Rumpel-Stilts-Ken" is a first-born child. The lady who benefits from Rumpel-Stilts-Ken's powers never even contemplates breaking her vow, although in a dreamlike way she does temporarily forget it. When the little man returns for his prize, the only alternatives are either to discover his name within three days or pay the consequence with living flesh.

The equivalence of word and flesh, which (as in the folk tale examples) threatens to entail the sacrifice of a child, is of course also a fundamental Christian myth. And as the Incarnate Word has in Christianity a gracious aspect, so in secular analogues the potentially menacing word may also be revealed at last as benign: a divine, rather than a diabolical, literalism. Shakespeare exploits such a reshuffling in various ways. In *Macbeth* the Witches' prophecies, which seem to portend good to Macbeth and therefore harm to the agents of grace, are fulfilled in the most natural—which in this case is also the literal—way; the rising of a wood becomes a simple military strategy, a man not born of woman is merely one delivered by Caesarian section. The bathos of the prophecies' fulfillment signals an alternate movement from the movement into the sphere of the binding word: in *Macbeth* Shakespeare takes us from the murky world of language's mystery back to the bright light of common human intercourse. In *The Winter's Tale,* the oracle delivered after the trial that condemns Hermione, that "the King shall live without an heir if that which is lost be not found" (3.2.134–36), is doubly fulfilled in the return both of Perdita (whose name makes her the essence of lostness) and of Hermione. Hermione's response to the accusatory, jealous Leontes, "You speak a language that I understand not" (3.2.80), signals the disjoining of two languages, one diabolical and one benign, which are reunited, to the accompaniment of music, at the familial reunion prophesied by the riddling oracle.

So the power of literalism can be either diabolical or divine, and it may at times be difficult to tell the one from the other. Such power is frequently contained in names, prophecies, riddles, oaths, contracts, legal codes and judgments: in any of these specialized uses of language a potentially dangerous or a divine autonomy may be invested in words which can then assume an existence independent of speaker or signatory. In Elizabethan drama, Marlowe's *Dr. Faustus* is perhaps the most striking treatment of diabolical literalism. Faustus, with his misplaced faith in outward symbols, makes a disastrous confusion between letter and spirit:

> Within this circle is Jehovah's name,
> Forward and backward anagrammatised:
> Th' abbreviated names of holy saints,
> Figures of every adjunct to the heavens,
> And characters of signs and erring stars,
> By which the spirits are enforced to rise.
>
> [1.3.5–10]

He assumes for himself, through this manipulation of symbols, an illusory power over the things symbolized; and not even Mephistophilis' teaching can free Faustus from his illusion. (Mephistophilis, with devilish pedantry, explains that the "conjuring speeches" were only the cause *"per accidens"* for his appearance to Faustus; the essential cause lies within.) Faustus' final terrible cry, "I'll burn my books," shows how little he has learned: to the very end he confuses the letter with the spirit. Thus, as frequently occurs in literary or in folk treatments of the theme, the literalist, aspiring to a diabolical status, has only succeeded in releasing those dangerous potentialities which—inept sorcerer's apprentice that in fact he is—work his own destruction.

Shylock is another presuming literalist, and in certain ways *The Merchant of Venice* is a comic analogue to the Faustian tragedy of misplaced faith in literalism. His "merry bond," which entails as a forfeit for late or nonpayment of the loan "an equal pound / Of [Antonio's] fair flesh, to be cut off and taken / In what part of [his] body" (1.3.145–47) pleases Shylock, is clearly a fairy-tale motif. But Shakespeare is the supreme artistic opportunist; here, he manages to retain the fairy-tale implausibility that the bond has in his sources (especially *Zelauto* and *Il Pecorone*) while at the same time making it dramatically acceptable in his relatively more "realistic" dramatic universe. He frankly confesses, indeed lets Shylock exult in, the preposterousness of the bond, thereby forestalling the audience's rational objections to it. When Bassanio demurs at the bond, Shylock presses the matter in a way that should fool no one, but to which no one could reasonably take exception either:

> O father Abram, what these Christians are,
> Whose own hard dealings teaches them suspect
> The thoughts of others! Pray you tell me this,—
> If he should break his day what should I gain
> By the exaction of the forfeiture?
> A pound of man's flesh taken from a man,
> Is not so estimable, profitable neither
> As flesh of muttons, beefs, or goats,—I say
> To buy his favour, I extend this friendship,—
> If he will take it, so,—if not, adieu,
> And for my love I pray you wrong me not.
>
> [1.3.156–66]

Here, it seems, is the eminently reasonable man, so secure in his knowledge of the boundaries between the quotidian and the marvellous that in all good fellowship he can make "merry sport" of such nonsense as a bond for a pound of flesh.

But even if we had not already heard in an aside of Shylock's desire to catch Antonio on the hip and "feed fat the ancient grudge I bear him" (1.3.42), there are indications in this very speech that we are in fact dealing with a diabolical literalist. The pedantic redundancy in the line "A pound of man's flesh taken from a man," the excessive specificity of the doubling "not so estimable, profitable neither," and the enumeration of "flesh of muttons, beefs, or goats," are characteristic rhetorical habits of the man who will later "crave the law, / The penalty and forfeit of his bond," demanding the precise measure "so nominated in the bond" (4.1.202–203, 255).

The domestication of the monstrous achieved by Shylock's show of reasonableness brings to mind the nearly insane specificity of some actual legal proceedings. It was not a fairy-tale monster but England's Lord Chief Justice who passed on Sir Walter Raleigh the formal sentence

> That you shall be had from hence to the place whence you came, there to remain until the day of execution; and from thence you shall be drawn upon the hurdle through the open streets to the place of execution, there to be hanged and cut down alive, and your body shall be opened, your heart and bowels plucked out, and your privy members cut off, and thrown into the fire before your eyes; then your head is to be stricken from your body, and your body shall be divided into four quarters, to be disposed of at the king's pleasure.

Such legal specificity leaves nothing to chance—no loopholes, as the expression has it—and that very quality of absoluteness is what makes the courtroom potentially a place of terror even to the innocent. The judicial sentence puts us at the linguistic border between ordinary reality and surreality, public truths and private fantasies, where the merest slip of the tongue may serve to condemn us.

That borderline is easily crossed. Along with the possible sources for *The Merchant of Venice,* Geoffrey Bullough records a note found in an Elizabethan book and probably written by its owner, Stephen Batman—an author of distinction, a Cambridge man and Doctor of Divinity. Batman sets down a hypothetical legal problem, apparently one he considered worthy of his professional consideration: "The note of a Jew wch for the interest of his money required a *li* of the man's flesh to whome he lent the money, the bonde forfeit and yet the Jew went withoute his purpose / the parti notwithstanding condemn'd by Lawe / the question whether he coulde cut the flesh withoute spilling of blood." [9] In such measured language the philosophical student plausibly conflates dream or fairy-tale horrors with our normal waking world. And so too, but with consummate artistry and perfect self-consciousness, does Shakespeare in this play.

There is thus much truth in Granville-Barker's assertions that "*The Merchant of Venice* is a fairy tale," and that "there is no more reality in Shylock's bond and the Lord of Belmont's will than in Jack and the Beanstalk." [10] But his dismissive tone is misleading, and it is worth pausing to consider one other "fairy tale" element beside those of the binding word and the flesh-forfeit. In myth and folk tale, things tend to come in threes. The lack of a name is tripled in "Nicht Nought Nothing," and in that story the unfortunate parents twice try to mislead the giant with a substitute child before giving up their own on the third occasion; the young man then goes on to complete, with the aid of the giant's fair daughter, three impossible tasks—the last of which, incidentally, demands from his helpmeet the sacrifice of numerous fingers and toes. And to glance quickly at some of the most familiar old tales, there are three wishes, three bears, three sons (of whom the most foolish finds a golden goose, to which there soon become inseparably attached three sisters), three nights of spinning, three days to guess the name. And from a different kind of source we recall the three temptations, the three days from Crucifixion to Resurrection, and the three members of the Trinity itself.

9. Geoffrey Bullough, ed., *Narrative and Dramatic Sources of Shakespeare* (London, 1957), 1 : 452.

10. *Prefaces to Shakespeare* (Princeton, 1946), 1 : 335.

In his specific sources Shakespeare encountered this sort of archetypal tripling. In the *Gesta Romanorum* he found the three caskets, and in *Il Pecorone* he found the thrice-ventured-for Lady of Belmonte. One significant change he made was to divide that venturing among three different suitors: in *Il Pecorone* it is a single feckless young man who has three attempts. And then to these triplets he added others. Now there are three different trials, that of the casket, that in the Venetian courtroom, and the final one of the rings. There are three thousand ducats loaned for three months. There are three couples united at the end—united, I would add, in the tripartite dance of the Graces, in which the lone Antonio—"the semblance of [Portia's] soul" because he is "the bosom lover" of her lord—also has a place. Through these many triplings Shakespeare increases our sense that the pattern is deeply implicated in the very structure of his play. He keeps his borrowings from the old tales, adds to them and deepens them with a sure sense of the potentialities, even approaching a Christian mystery, in the convention. He retains the sense of wonder the convention evokes, while increasing the sense of comic inevitability entailed in the multiplying of threes.

In the Venetian court the literalist apparently finds his perfect arena. There is at least the show of a reason why this court must be the "strict court" it is—and it is significant that, with the momentary exception of Bassanio's plea to have the law wrested by personal authority, everyone agrees with that reason. Venice is the world's chief commercial center; Antonio, the merchant at the center of that center, puts the case for strictness most clearly:

> The duke cannot deny the course of law:
> For the commodity that strangers have
> With us in Venice, if it be denied,

> Will much impeach the justice of the state,
> Since that the trade and profit of the city
> Consisteth of all nations.
>
> [3.3.26–31]

But while the reason is put in terms of commerce, it is not a matter merely of commercial expediency. Relatively history-bound and particular as the Venetians' case for strict justice is, it is nonetheless a version of the case put in Heaven by the embodied figure of Justicia. To break or bend the law is to do violence to the fundamental nature of the state itself or, as Antonio puts it in a heavily weighted phrase, "the justice of the state"—to that, in other words, which makes the state just. The necessary rigidity of Venetian law guarantees that everyone will be treated the same under the law, of which the law of contracts is only one case. Therein lies the law's strength but also, of course, its weakness—a partial paradox clearly expressed by Hooker in his *Laws of Ecclesiastical Polity:*

> we see in contracts and other dealings which daily pass between man and man, that, to the utter undoing of some, many things by strictness of law may be done, which equity and honest meaning forbiddeth. Not that the law is unjust, but unperfect; nor equity against, but above, the law, binding men's consciences in things which law cannot reach unto.[11]

The claims of "equity" are several times pressed in Shakespeare's courtroom; but each time they are countered by Shylock's recourse to the more powerful—because, unlike the claims of equity, they are codified—claims of common law. The Duke first urges a "gentle answer" (4.1.34) from Shylock, who counters with his demand for "the due and forfeit" of his bond: "If you deny it, let the danger light /

11. Book 5, chap. 9, sect. 3; quoted in John W. Dickinson, "Renaissance Equity and *Measure for Measure*," *SQ*, 13 (1962) : 288.

Upon your charter and your city's freedom" (38–39). Echoing Scripture (James 2:13), the Duke asks "How shalt thou hope for mercy, rend'ring none?" (88). And again Shylock responds with the Venetians' own principle: "If you deny me, fie upon your law! / There is no force in the decrees of Venice. / I stand for judgment,—answer, shall I have it?" (101–03).

This is the impasse that Portia finds when she arrives disguised as Balthazar, old Bellario's supposed protégé. As we have seen, her speech on "the quality of mercy" does nothing, in any practical way, to break the impasse. In fact one of the functions of the speech is to *increase* the sense of this court's absolute legal strictness, and it suggests another reason why Shakespeare has so created it. Her explicit reference to Christian doctrine, especially the Lord's Prayer ("We do pray for mercy, / And that same prayer, doth teach us all to render / The deeds of mercy" [196–98]), lifts the dispute to the universal level. And as only God's mercy can free us from the just sentence passed against mankind, so in Venice's strict court only an act of mercy can mitigate the rigor of law. The absence of any enforceable concept of equity allows the Venetian law's excessive literalism to suggest the most general and inexorable law of all, the law of mortality; and it therefore also increases our desire for some mitigation of that universal rigor.

It is frequently alleged that Portia uses the merest trick to exculpate Antonio and defeat Shylock's claim; but a "trick" from one perspective may be the most amazing grace from another. In an apocryphal trial widely known throughout the medieval period, the so-called *Processus Belial,* the devil appears in court demanding that mankind, forfeited to him at the fall, be delivered up to him. The devil's argument is essentially the one made in another trial by God's own daughters, Truth and Justice: God cannot preserve mankind without violating His own edict, His own Word. In the *Processus Belial* it is the Virgin Mary who appears for the defense, arguing the counter-claim of mercy, and thus driving the devil, defeated, from the court.[12] And from the stringency of Venetian law, as it appears in our play at the time judgment is about to be rendered, only a similarly miraculous intervention would seem capable of releasing the law's destined sacrifice.

Shylock's literalism is only one case of several in the play in which language is perverted from its properly benign service. False reasoning and deceptive rhetoric are related to that perversion of language I have called diabolical literalism—and before going on to consider Portia's legal procedure we should pause over some examples of language pressed into the service of falsehood.

Launcelot Gobbo, trying "confusions" on his blind father, is a comically false reasoner with a suitably twisted language. We have seen how Launcelot confuses carnal concerns with spiritual: he will leave the service of the Jew because the Christian can give rarer liveries and larger suppers. It is not only the devil who (as Antonio says of Shylock) "can cite Scripture for his purpose" (1.3.93); as act 3, scene 5 begins, Launcelot is citing Exodus 20:5 to Jessica: "Yes truly, for look you, the sins of the father are to be laid upon the children." Launcelot does indeed "speak [his] agitation of the matter" when he concludes that Jessica (who therefore should "be o' good cheer") is damned. Jessica's less agitated conclusion is in keeping with a doctrine enunciated in 1 Corinthians 8 : 14: "I shall be sav'd by my husband,—he hath made me a Christian!" (3.5.17–18). But even that conclusion comes short of the truth in supposing salvation to be a matter of legal niceties. As the Apostle to the Gentiles writes concerning the Jews' ultimate redemption, "if the casting away of them be the reconciling of the worlde, what shal the receiving be, but life from the dead?" (Rom. 11 : 15).

12. John D. Rea, "Shylock and the *Processus Belial*," *PQ*, 8 (1929) : 311–13.

Launcelot is also worried about the rise in the price of hogs with all "this making of Christians" (3.5.21): a wonderful confusion of carnal matters and spiritual. And perhaps that confusion explains the otherwise mysterious accusation brought by Lorenzo that "the Moor is with child" by Launcelot (3.5.35–36); it simply reinforces Launcelot's association, however vital and amusing, with the world of the flesh. Without loading too much matter on the slender comedy of young Master Gobbo, we can at least say that one of his functions is repeatedly to twist spiritual truths towards the carnal—to be associated with the flesh in a light mood as Shylock is in his darker way. Launcelot's amusing misuse of language shows Lorenzo "How every fool can play upon the word!" (3.5.40), while it acts for the audience as a foil to set off other foolish abusers of reason and language in the play.

When Bassanio, in one of the play's other "trials," is about to make his choice of caskets, he reflects on how "The world is still deceiv'd with ornament—":

> In law, what plea so tainted and corrupt,
> But being season'd with a gracious voice,
> Obscures the show of evil? In religion,
> What damned error but some sober brow
> Will bless it, and approve it with a text,
> Hiding the grossness with fair ornament?
>
> [3.2.74–80]

This warning against deceptive rhetoric, which Bassanio himself heeds when he correctly makes his choice of lead's "paleness," is of course relevant to his two unfortunate predecessors in Belmont, Morocco and Arragon; and it is also relevant to Shylock's various pleas. The theme of deceptive rhetoric therefore serves as one of several links between the Venetian and the Belmont plot-lines.

The arguments of the three contestants for Portia are more elaborate and subtle, as their task is more difficult, than the arguments in Shakespeare's probable source. In the *Gesta Romanorum* (a version of which, including the story of the casket-choice, appeared in 1595), the riddling inscriptions are, "Who so chooseth mee shall finde that he deserveth," "Who so chooseth mee shall finde that his nature desireth," and "Who so chooseth mee shall finde that God hath disposed for him." Only the first riddle corresponds to one in *The Merchant of Venice:* "Who chooseth me, shall get as much as he deserves" (2.7.7). The two other inscriptions substituted by Shakespeare[13]—"Who chooseth me, shall gain what many men desire," and "Who chooseth me, must give and hazard all he hath" (2.7.5, 9)—make the contest rather more difficult than the one successfully completed by the Maiden in the *Gesta Romanorum.* They also give ampler scope for subtleties and sleights of rhetoric.

Both Morocco and Arragon give short shrift to the lead casket with its threatening inscription. But Morocco's rejection of it is accompanied by a sufficiently plausible argument, and is in that respect typical of the rhetorical subtlety Shakespeare has given the casket-trial. "A golden mind," says Morocco, "stoops not to shows of dross" (2.7.20). This is perfectly reasonable—so long as one can distinguish true gold from fool's gold. But Morocco's blindness in the matter of spiritual evaluation is evident from his first comically blustering reaction to the lead casket's inscription:

> Must give,—for what? for lead, hazard for lead!
> This casket threatens—men that hazard all
> Do it in hope of fair advantages:
> A golden mind stoops not to shows of dross,
> I'll then nor give nor hazard aught for lead.
>
> [2.7.17–21]

It is less the "dross" than the demanded action, the giving, that Morocco immediately recoils from. Indeed men that

13. Or it is possible that the change in casket-inscriptions derives from the putative lost source-play—and that, possibly, is the one Gosson refers to as *The Iew:* see note 4, chapter 1.

hazard may receive fair advantages; but in the truly important matters of charity and faith those advantages will not be theirs if the desire for a good return has motivated the hazarding. Morocco absurdly fails to see that of the three caskets only the lead one allows the hazarding of "all" that could bring the gain there really is in giving. And Morocco, like Arragon later, confuses the outside with the inside—"*shows* of dross" with real dross, the literal with the spiritual. His confusion, plausibly disguised by his rhetoric's "fair ornament" of half-truths, is like that of the young man in the Gospel who, claiming to have kept all the commandments, asked Christ what more he must do to have eternal life:

> Iesus said vnto him, If thou wilt be perfite, go, sel that thou hast, & giue it to the poore, and thou shalt haue treasure in heauen, and come and followe me. / And when the yong man heard that saying, he went away sorowful: for he had great possesions. [Matt. 19 : 21–22]

Morocco will depart sorrowful—and celibate too—because, unlike Antonio, Portia, and Bassanio, he rejects the invitation to become a part of the tripartite dance of gracious giving.

Specious reasoning also determines Morocco's choice of the gold over the silver casket. The silver, with its inscription "Who chooseth me, shall get as much as he deserves," has a powerful claim on Morocco who, weighing his value with an even hand, finds that in his own estimate he does deserve "enough" (2.7.25–27). Still, he must consider whether the vast "enough" that he deserves will "extend so far as to the lady" (28).

> And yet to be afeard of my deserving
> Were but a weak disabling of myself.
> As much as I deserve,—why that's the lady.
> I do in birth deserve her, and in fortunes,

In graces, and in qualities of breeding:
But more than these, in love I do deserve,—
What if I stray'd no further, but chose here?
Let's see once more this saying grav'd in gold . . . .
[2.7.29–36]

Portia's father (we have learned from Nerissa) "was ever virtuous, and holy men at their death have good inspirations": therefore the lead casket will "never be chosen by any rightly, but one who you shall rightly love" (1.2.27–28, 31–32). The Portia whose knowledge of "the quality of mercy" is perfect, could never "rightly love" the man whom we see here so judiciously weighing his own just deserts. Hamlet's tendentious question to Polonius, "Use every man after his desert, and who shall 'scape whipping?" (*Ham.* 2.2.529–30), rudely makes the same point that Portia so much more elegantly makes, "That in the course of justice, none of us / Should see salvation." Morocco, having "stray'd" thus far beyond the lead casket will, on second consideration, stray still further to the gold; and he will never doubt the validity of his fundamentally specious standards of judgment.

Morocco is (to borrow Gosson's phrase) a "worldly chooser." The fact that he is black—an alien like Shylock—makes Shakespeare's treatment of his wrongheadedness more interesting. Morocco's assumption of self-worth is admirable, but the conclusions he draws from the assumption are nonetheless false. Neither his complexion, nor his birth, fortunes, graces, and qualities of breeding (the things Morocco prides himself on) disable him as Portia's suitor; he is, in all these things, no doubt a fine person—but he is blind to the fundamental truths to which the caskets' inscriptions and their contents point. As he proceeds to consider the gold casket—"Who chooseth me, shall gain what many men desire"—he reveals, through his own exaggerated rhetoric, that his worldliness is in fact idolatry:

Why that's the lady, all the world desires her.
From the four corners of the earth they come
To kiss this shrine, this mortal breathing saint.
The Hyrcanian deserts, and the vasty wilds
Of wide Arabia are as thoroughfares now
For princes to come view fair Portia.
The watery kingdom, whose ambitious head
Spets in the face of heaven, is no bar
To stop the foreign spirits, but they come
As o'er a brook to see fair Portia.

[2.7.38–47]

The scroll he finds within the death's head's hollow eye might as well be describing his verse as the golden casket: " 'Gilded tombs do worms infold' " (68). The hyperbolic lushness of his speech is perfectly suited to the man who forgets that " 'All that glisters is not gold' " (65), and who foolishly (if with a surface brilliance) calls Portia a "mortal breathing saint" and "an angel in a golden bed" (58). Portia is neither saint nor angel but a lovely young woman, and in charity to her we may assume that her farewell to Morocco, "Let all of his complexion choose me so," refers less to his skin than to his temperament and habits of mind.

Arragon's choosing is a shorter business and, in its abuses of language and logic, a funnier. Rather than Morocco's too-expansive rhetoric, Arragon's is brisk, assertive, and ludicrously (because so wrongheadedly) sententious. His rejection of the lead casket takes only a single line: "You shall look fairer ere I give or hazard" (2.9.22); but to each of the other two caskets he devotes a passage remarkable for the way it draws a wrong conclusion from a reasonable premise. About the gold casket's legend, "Who chooseth me, shall gain what many men desire," Arragon reasons

that 'many' may be meant
By the fool multitude that choose by show,
Not learning more than the fond eye doth teach,

Which pries not to th' interior, but like the martlet
Builds in the weather on the outward wall,
Even in the force and road of casualty.
I will not choose what many men desire. . . .

[2.9.25–31]

This refusal to "choose by show" or to trust what "the fond eye doth teach" is admirable. Unfortunately for Arragon, we have just heard him dismiss the lead casket because it does not "look fairer": between Arragon's actions and his words there is an inconsistency which warns us that his didactic tone makes him one of the play's false teachers.

The conclusion he draws from his sententious warning against choosing "by show" lets us pry to his interior:

I will not choose what many men desire,
Because I will not jump with common spirits,
And rank me with the barbarous multitudes.

[31–33]

Pride motivates Arragon's rejection of the gold casket. He is moved as much "by show" as are those "barbarous multitudes" he disdains; and he is all the more culpable for the way he twists an initial truth into his concluding falsehood. Arragon's fastidious concern not to seem one of the "fool multitude" brings to mind the warning in 1 Corinthians 3 : 18: "Let no man deceiue him self. If anie man among you seme to be wise in this worlde, let him be a foole, that he may be wise."

Arragon's pride makes his choice of the silver casket inevitable: " 'Who chooseth me shall get as much as he deserves,' " the inscription says, and Arragon is ready to "assume desert" (2.9.51). But again the wrong choice is preceded by a sufficiently plausible show of reason. Indeed this vain "blinking idiot" (54) takes it upon himself to be a scourge of the times, inveighing against just the sorts of error of which he stands self-convicted:

let none presume
To wear an undeserved dignity:
O that estates, degrees, and offices
Were not deriv'd corruptly, and that clear honour
Were purchas'd by the merit of the wearer!—
How many then should cover that stand bare!
How many be commanded that command!
How much low peasantry would then be gleaned
From the true seed of honour! and how much honour
Pick'd from the chaff and ruin of the times,
To be new-varnish'd!

[2.9.39–49]

As Portia says in her farewell to Arragon, "O these deliberate fools! when they do choose, / They have the wisdom by their wit to lose" (2.9.80–81). Arragon, who to the end refuses to "appear" a fool (73), is the epitome of worldly wisdom, self-deceived and incapable of coming by reason to the open truths of the spirit.

It is essential to Shakespeare's overall scheme that both Morocco and Arragon be allowed at least a degree of plausibility. While every convention of fairy tale and myth lets us rest assured that the first two of the three suitors will fail, and that (as Nerissa has assured us) their failure will be sufficient proof of their unacceptability, still in their speeches we can momentarily be seduced into taking rhetorical dross for gold. And those partial seductions by falsehood's goodly outside (1.3.97) should serve the audience as preparation for the more difficult test awaiting them in Shylock's rhetoric. The successsion of scenes here is worth noting: in 2.9, Arragon makes his choice and is dismissed, and the scene ends with "an ambassador of love" bringing the news of Bassanio's approach; the next scene, 3.1, brings us "news on the Rialto," and includes Shylock's rhetorical masterpiece, "Hath not a Jew eyes"; in 3.2, Bassanio makes his choice, and both he and Portia are allowed lengthy, sententious speeches: the scene concludes with the reading of Antonio's letter, bringing news of his apparently fatal ill-luck, and Bassanio's departure for Venice; 3.3 is the short scene giving us Shylock at his most implacable, repeatedly bidding "Goaler, look to him," and "I'll have my bond." The scenic juxtapositions bring the worlds of Venice and Belmont successively closer, binding the two plot strands (casket-choice and pound of flesh) unobtrusively and inextricably. And the rhetorical set pieces in the scenes—Arragon's, Shylock's, Bassanio's, and Portia's—are made subtly counterpointing and mutually informative.

Morocco, in his first appearance, has delivered a speech which begins like an eloquent plea for universal toleration:

> Mislike me not for my complexion,
> The shadowed livery of the burnish'd sun,
> To whom I am a neighbour, and near bred.
>
> [2.1.1–3]

But almost immediately the speech turns in a quite different direction. Morocco's orotund verse in fact makes a claim for his *superiority* to other mere mortals. Indeed he is so blinded by pride that he commits an obvious error of logic: having asked Portia to dismiss the question of his "complexion," he goes on immediately to offer the challenge:

> Bring me the fairest creature northward born,
> Where Phoebus' fire scarce thaws the icicles,
> And let us make incision for your love,
> To prove *whose blood is reddest, his or mine.*
>
> [4–7]

And from that sanguinary boast he immediately modulates into self-praise of "this aspect of mine," which "the best-regarded virgins of our clime / Have loved. . . ." (10–11). Morocco's self-infatuation is comically absurd. But when, several scenes later, Shylock too asks us to "make incision" ("if you prick us do we not bleed?"), the comedy is gone;

and the rhetorical sleight is so far concealed that one might easily take his "Hath not a Jew eyes" speech as a plea on behalf of brotherhood rather than a defense of murderous revenge.

I suspect that as a school set piece the speech is often recalled, not from its beginning or in its full context, but from the point where the rhetorical questioning begins. In fact, the speech is Shylock's response to a prior rhetorical question: "thou wilt not take his flesh,—what's that good for?" (3.1.46). And the supposedly eloquent plea that follows is an elaboration of Shylock's brutal answer: "To bait fish withal,—if it will feed nothing else, it will feed my revenge" (47–48)—where the earlier comedy of Morocco's claim to have redder blood than other men is darkened into this intimation of cannibalism. The speech is the culminating example of language turned, however brilliantly, into a tool of deceit. It is important to know those parts of the speech which do command respect, but also to understand the sophistical wrongness of the whole:

> To bait fish withal,—if it will feed nothing else, it will feed my revenge; he hath disgrac'd me, and hind'red me half a million, laugh'd at my losses, mock'd at my gains, scorned my nation, thwarted my bargains, cooled my friends, heated mine enemies,—and what's his reason? I am a Jew. Hath not a Jew eyes? hath not a Jew hands, organs, dimensions, senses, affections, passions? fed with the same food, hurt with the same weapons, subject to the same diseases, healed by the same means, warmed and cooled by the same winter and summer as a Christian is?—if you prick us do we not bleed? if you tickle us do we not laugh? if you poison us do we not die? and if you wrong us shall we not revenge?—if we are like you in the rest, we will resemble you in that. If a Jew wrong a Christian, what is his humility? revenge! If a Christian wrong a

> Jew, what should his sufferance be by Christian example?—why revenge! The villainy you teach me I will execute, and it shall go hard but I will better the instruction. [3.1.47–66]

Morocco's error was to assume racial superiority; Shylock's is almost the reverse: he reduces humanity to its lowest common denominator and perversely finds at that level the touches of nature that make the whole world kin. But the most remarkable aspect of the speech is the leap it makes from brotherhood to barbarity.

Shylock's rhetorical strategy makes that leap almost imperceptible. The rhetoric is worth pausing over, in part because the very familiarity of the speech puts us in danger of missing some of the things that make it extraordinary, and also because the history of responses to Shylock indicates that its seductiveness has not been ineffectual.[14] That seductiveness is all the more extraordinary for the way the speech begins: the initial statement about revenge—that Antonio's flesh will serve "to bait fish withal,—if it will feed nothing else, it will feed my revenge"—is so melodramatically horrific that it makes the stunt that follows a tour de force. Shylock allows himself to start from the tactically worst position, then gradually converts his defiant loathsomeness into a seemingly justifiable, even a righteous, position.

Between the initial statement about revenge and the final

14. It is not necessary to document the extent to which Shylock's speech has charmed audiences and critics. The Variorum quotes Victor Hugo, one powerful example to show how well Shylock is able to make revenge seem an appropriate response to an injury: "This sublime imprecation is the most eloquent plea that the human voice has ever dared to utter for a despised race. Whatsoever be the denoument, it is hereby justified. Let Shylock be as implacable as he may, assuredly he will no more than equal his instruction. Even granting that he obtains it, a pound of Antonio's flesh will never outweigh, in the scales of reprisal, the millions of corpses heaped in the Christian shambles by a butchery of thirteen centuries."

one, in which revenge has been equated with Christian "humility" and made to seem a common human inevitability, there comes, first, Shylock's statement of the wrongs he has suffered from Antonio. And we must admit that Shylock has been wronged. Leo Kirschbaum objects that even in this part of his speech Shylock's vocabulary is self-condemning: " 'losses,' 'gains,' 'bargains,' and 'half a million' recall [Shylock's] villainous business morality." [15] We will take up the question of that "business morality"—along with the question of usury—elsewhere; here we need say only that even if Kirschbaum's point is valid, it still leaves out other crucial matters in Shylock's indictment of Antonio: "he hath disgraced me . . . scorned my nation . . . cooled my friends . . . heated mine enemies." Nor is this merely Shylock's invention; we have heard Antonio himself, with unrepentent malice, proudly admit that he has acted and will continue to act uncharitably toward Shylock: "I am as like to call thee [cur] again, / To spet on thee again, to spurn thee too" (1.3.125–26). It is such an admission and such actions that make Shylock's claim about a "Christian example" carry what weight it does.

Shylock's catalogue of Antonio's past injuries to him accumulates speed and force as it progresses. The first three phrases are drawn out in length by their syntactical variety, with an auxiliary verb in the first ("he *hath* disgrac'd me"), a conjunction in the second ("*and* hind'red me half a million"), and a preposition in the third ("laugh'd *at* my losses"). But then the parallelism becomes more rigid, first through the firm establishment of an asyndetic construction and then, after the phrase "mock'd at my gains," through the perfect syntactical symmetry of the last four phrases. The effect is an accelerating speech rhythm which makes its sudden interruption, "—and what's his reason?" startle us into renewed attention. And the attention is fully rewarded by the next four monosyllables: "I am a Jew."

15. Kirschbaum, *Character and Characterization,* p. 24.

That declaration, which may have been as arresting to an Elizabethan as it is to us who survive the Holocaust, and as emotionally overburdened with its weight of pride, pain, defiance, and pleading, introduces the great series of rhetorical questions. A proper wariness of sentimentality should not blunt for us the point of those questions, nor should an attempt to be mindful of the Elizabethan ethos conflict with the assent those questions demand. But the assent, notice, is only to a lowest common denominator of physical facts; [16] and possibly because their claim is so undeniable we may be seduced into acquiescing in Shylock's sudden, unsignalled descent from truism to sophistry: "and if you wrong us shall we not revenge?—if we are like you in the rest, we will resemble you in that."

All "the rest" in which Jew and Christian are alike has been, till this point in Shylock's speech, a subvolitional matter: bleeding when pricked, laughing when tickled, dying when poisoned. Now, without warning, Shylock has introduced an entirely different matter, one that *is* volitional (although he tries to make revenge seem a virtually instinctive response) and capable of being judged according to ethical and theological standards. The conclusion to Shylock's speech is logically fallacious, confusing as it does unvolitional, instinctive, or purely physical matters with a matter of a totally different order: revenge. The fact that the speech is capable of eliciting an emotionally positive response despite its sophistry is testimony to Shylock's mastery of a diabolic rhetoric. But the logic of the speech remains unacceptable, as it is morally unacceptable too, whether judged by Christian or by Jewish standards.

That Shylock's attempt to justify deadly revenge is unacceptable by Jewish standards is an elementary point, but it still seems necessary to make it. For the Christian, the Old Law is the foundation of the New, and its moral essence is not abrogated but fulfilled in the New. But the

16. Cf. a similarly carnal argument at 4.1.47 ff.

Tables of the Law were, after all, given to Moses, whose people have never given them away. In Shylock's statement of universal oneness there is none of the spirit expressed, for instance, in the rhetorical questions of the Hebrew prophet Malachi: "Haue we not all one father? hathe not one God made vs?" (2 : 10). And in the final lesson of revenge that Shylock claims to have gleaned from "Christian example," an older lesson, taught to the Jews in Deuteronomy 32 : 35 and twice quoted by St. Paul, "Vengeance is mine: I wil repaye, saith the Lord" (Rom. 12 : 19; cf. Heb. 10 : 30), is completely forgotten.

The phrase "an eye for an eye, a tooth for a tooth" (Ex. 21 : 24, Lev. 24 : 20, Deut. 19 : 21) is certainly not an adequate epitome of Old Testament ethical teaching. And even that formula is often misunderstood, wrongly taken as if it were a license to savagery or as the Hebraic equivalent of Bacon's definition of revenge as "a kind of wild justice." In fact the Old Testament's "an eye for an eye" is the *opposite* of vengeful license.[17] St. Augustine's exegesis of the phrase would be acceptable as rabbinic halakah: "*Moderation* is signified by these words, so that the penalty may not be greater than the injury. And this," writes Augustine, "is the beginning of peace."[18] Thus, from either a Jewish or a Christian perspective, Shylock's immoderate thirst for revenge disqualifies him from the role, into which some critics have tried to cast him, as the representative of a "race."

St. Augustine, stressing the fulfilling of the Old Law in

17. Gordon W. Zeeveld, *Temper of Shakespeare's Thought,* says that "the Jew represents in an exaggerated form *the revenge which characterized the Old Law* (p. 150, my italics; and cf. p. 155: "the Old Law of revenge"). This is inaccurate, by either Jewish or Christian standards. From the Christian perspective—or the Shakespearean—the failure of the Old Law is not that it demands "revenge" (it doesn't), but that it offers no means for salvation through grace.

18. St. Augustine, *Commentary on the Lord's Sermon on the Mount,* in *Fathers of the Church,* 11 : 80; my italics.

the New, goes on to say that "a man is showing some forgiveness if he retaliates with an injury that is exactly equivalent to the injury he has received, for a guilty man deserves a penalty that is not the exact equivalent of the injury which an innocent man has received from him." Therefore "an eye for an eye, a tooth for a tooth" is, according to Augustine, "not a severe justice, but a merciful one." From his perspective, however, it is still only a "preparatory justice," for "to have absolutely no wish for any such retribution—that is perfect peace." The Old Testament's preparatory justice "has been brought to perfection by Him who came, not to destroy the Law, but to fulfill it" (81).

Shylock's "Hath not a Jew eyes" speech is only one example of the way he misuses language, making it a tool of deceit and enlisting it, finally, in the diabolic literalism of his flesh-bond. However, linguistic sleights (as well as the abuses of mere stupidity) are by no means a Shylockian monopoly. Morocco and Arragon are deeply implicated; Launcelot Gobbo is, too. Even Bassanio, whose ultimate moral fitness is proven by his choice of the lead casket, is not wholly innocent in this regard. Although he himself protests that "what follows is pure innocence" (1.1.145), his long-winded request for a loan from Antonio, with its dubious analogy between going doubly into debt and a childhood trick in archery (1.1.140–52), shows that Bassanio has things to learn about the relationship of rhetoric to right-reason, and of words to love. Antonio chides him:

> You know me well, and herein spend but time
> To wind about my love with circumstance,
> And out of doubt you do me now more wrong
> In making question of my uttermost
> Than if you had made waste of all I have:
> Then do but say to me what I should do
> That in your knowledge may by me be done,

> And I am prest unto it: therefore speak.
> [1.1.153–60]

But Bassanio is an apt pupil; and in his own succeeding responses to requests for aid he enacts an increased awareness of generosity's ungarrulous spontaneity. When the Gobbos, for instance, struggle with a recalcitrant language to tell of Launcelot's "infection sir, (as one would say) to serve" him, Bassanio quickly answers, "I know thee well, thou hast obtain'd thy suit" (2.2.119, 137)—where the rhetorical exuberance of his pun on the word "suit" (meaning the "rare new liveries" Launcelot wants, as well as his request to serve) keeps decorum with the comic situation. And when Gratiano announces, "I have a suit to you," Bassanio answers unhesitatingly "You have obtain'd it" (2.2.169).

Gratiano himself is a harder case, but useful for us since he shows how egregiously the nominal Christians of the play can err—and how, therefore, the play's parabolic aspect does not depend upon a simple polarity of good Christians versus bad Jews. Bassanio, who will be accompanied throughout his trials by this joking, maladroit Gratiano, says of him:

> Gratiano speaks an infinite deal of nothing (more than any man in all Venice), his reasons are as two grains of wheat hid in two bushels of chaff: you shall seek all day ere you find them, and when you have them, they are not worth the search. [1.1.114–18]

It is, in fact, no easy trick to speak "an infinite deal of nothing": such an unimaginable multiplication of sheer absence would move Gratiano's rhetoric toward that diabolic sphere where language, unleashing its full potential for paradox and pun, becomes dangerously autonomous. In fact, however, Gratiano is not ingenious enough for that, although he does remain addicted to the sweet smoke of rhetoric through the very last words of the play. The paradox of Gratiano's linguistic "nothing" is a moral one, that in speaking falsehood (which refers to no real thing) he is speaking *the thing that is not.*

And when we first hear him speak his moral "nothing" he is speaking it with a sententiousness (albeit jovial enough) that marks him out as one of the play's false teachers. His diagnosis of Antonio's condition repeats, in brief, the errors of Salerio and Solanio:

> You look not well, Signior Antonio,
> You have too much respect upon the world:
> They lose it that do buy it with much care,—
> Believe me you are marvellously chang'd.
>
> [1.1.73–76]

Antonio's disclaimer is heard by Gratiano only as a kind of dramatic cue: if every man must play a part (and Antonio's is a sad one), Gratiano will eagerly "play the fool" (79):

> With mirth and laughter let old wrinkles come,
> And let my liver rather heat with wine
> Than my heart cool with mortifying groans.
>
> [80–82]

Gratiano's excessiveness in the way of mirth and laughter makes him the direct antithesis of Shylock, who is notably deficient in those departments. And when, at the trial, Gratiano capers about, taunting Shylock and exulting in his discomfiture, this excessiveness (which in certain circumstances can be attractive enough) is revealed in its more repulsive aspect. Gratiano's inclusion in the harmony of the fifth act's close—and the fact, indeed, that Shakespeare has allowed his final pun to bear a serious, summarizing import of which the speaker himself may be unaware—shows how capacious that harmony is, accommodating even as discordant a note as Gratiano, and so eventually perhaps even Shylock, within its full diapason.

Having incorrectly diagnosed the cause of Antonio's melancholy state, Gratiano goes blithely on to lecture him against fishing with "this melancholy bait / For this fool gudgeon, this opinion" of being "reputed wise / For saying nothing" (1.1.96–102). His speech is sufficiently witty in itself, and contains what is possibly the play's most amusing misuse of scriptural allusion: referring to Matthew 5 : 22, "And whosoever shal say, Foole, shal be worthie to be punished with hel fyre," Gratiano says of those whose silence makes them seem wise, that "If they should speak, [they] would almost damn those ears / Which (hearing them) would call their brothers fools" (1.1.98–99). But Gratiano's wit here is also a kind of insouciance, self-involved and heedless of Antonio's real needs.

The hypocrisy he warns Antonio against is one Gratiano claims to be adept in himself. When Bassanio agrees to let Gratiano accompany him to Belmont, Bassanio gently chides him for being "too wild, too rude, and bold of voice" (2.2.172) and bids him

take pain
To allay with some cold drops of modesty
Thy skipping spirit, lest through thy wild behaviour
I be misconst'red in the place I go to,
And lose my hopes.

[2.2.176–180]

Gratiano's response is an exuberant promise to act the perfect hypocrite:

Signior Bassanio, hear me—
If I do not put on a sober habit,
Talk with respect, and swear but now and then,
Wear prayer-books in my pocket, look demurely,
Nay more, while grace is saying hood mine eyes
Thus with my hat, and sigh and say "amen":
Use all the observance of civility

> Like one well studied in a sad ostent
> To please his grandam, never trust me more.
>
> [2.2.180–88]

But we do not, I think, feel that Gratiano is too terribly culpable, despite even this admission of his dishonesty. In action he is loyal to his friends, although lacking in charity to those who are not within that charmed circle. His levity has its repellent aspects. He is a limited human being, a lesser version of Bassanio and a foil—as well, perhaps, as a warning—to him. He is an appropriate, if unwitting, beneficiary of the unconstrainable mercy that gratuitously drops manna in the way of starving people.

The play's array of false teachers and abusers of language helps account for the extraordinary sententiousness of Portia's and Bassanio's speeches at the casket-choice. It is as though they had to counterbalance, here at the midway point of the action (3.2), the accumulating weight of error. No doubt the rhetorical heightening of their speeches is also theatrically necessary to make the static business of choosing seem to an audience a perilous trial. But the speeches should not therefore be dismissed as theatrical trickery or speech-day finery.

Portia's speech on music, for instance, may be a series of commonplaces; but it is also particularly relevant. It glances ahead to the music that is to be so prominent in the fifth act, and backward to Shylock's attempt to lock out the sound of "the drum / And the vile squealing of the wry-neck'd fife" (2.5.29–30). From such particular references, as well as from the harmonious structure of the play as a whole, Portia's speech gathers to itself increased vitality.

Her first thought is of loss:

> Let music sound while he doth make his choice,
> Then if he lose he makes a swan-like end,
> Fading in music. That the comparison

May stand more proper, my eye shall be the stream
And wat'ry death-bed for him.

[3.2.43–47]

Even in this highly mannered expression, Portia's creative way with language is apparent. The sufficiently conventional "swan-like end," for instance, is virtually enacted in the sounds of her lines, as the initial trochaic substitution makes "fading in music" the echo of its sense. She explicitly directs our attention to her creation of metaphors ("that the comparison may stand more proper"), and with her art thus openly confessed allows us to watch her in the act of embellishing the thought, neatly conflating tenor and vehicle by making her eye the carrier of the metaphoric swan. This "honest method" (as well, of course, as the intrinsic worth of what she is saying) distinguishes her rhetorical coloring from the deceitful "ornament" against which Bassanio declaims in his speech following hers.

Portia's next thought is a happier one: "he may win, / And what is music then?" (47–48). The comparisons that follow—to "the flourish, when true subjects bow / To a new-crowned monarch" and to "those dulcet sounds in break of day, / That creep into a dreaming bridegroom's ear / And summon him to marriage" (49–53)—bring together three realms; or rather bring *back* together, since it is only "whilst this muddy vesture of decay / Doth grossly close [us] in" (5.1.64–65) that the realms seem distinct rather than as various manifestations of a single thing. One realm is that of music itself; and this (as we will be told explicitly in act 5) is the divine realm, where each smallest orb in its motion makes a part of the music of the spheres. True subjects bowing to their new-made monarch introduces the civil realm, where men in their obedience to temporal rulers properly imitate the obedience of all creation to God. And the summons to marriage introduces an intimately private realm, but one in which the two individuals joined in a sacramental relationship again show the essential singleness of these apparently various realms: as Hymen sings in *As You Like It,* "Then is there mirth in heaven, / When earthly things made even / Atone together" (5.4.108–10). And throughout the speech, in the very act of metaphor-making itself, Portia in effect takes part in the same universal movement toward harmony that is suggested by her bringing together the realms comprehended by music, civil government, and marriage.

Portia's language in the speech that follows Bassanio's successful choice again insists on the singleness behind apparent diversity. Her role as a teacher has been alluded to twice in the scene: "I could," she has said to Bassanio, "teach you / How to choose right, but then I am forsworn" (3.2.10–11), and Bassanio, having changed Portia's "confess and live" into " 'confess and love' " (35), calls it "O happy torment, when my torturer / Doth teach me answers for deliverance" (37–38). But this teacher is glad simultaneously to be a learner. As she gives herself wholly to Bassanio, Portia calls herself "an unlesson'd girl, unschool'd, unpractised,"—

> Happy in this, she is not yet so old
> But she may learn; happier than this,
> She is not bred so dull but she can learn;
> Happiest of all, is that her gentle spirit
> Commits itself to yours to be directed. . . .
> [159–64]

The line that completes Portia's thought—"As from her lord, her governor, her king"—again creates a metaphoric joining of the state of matrimony with the well-ordered civil state. The master-servant relationship is made transferable as Portia continues in lines that glance also at the exchange of selves in love:

> But now I was the lord
> Of this fair mansion, master of my servants,

Queen o'er myself; and even now, but now,
This house, these servants, and this same myself
Are yours,—my lord's!

[167–71]

And in the final gesture of her speech Portia introduces the motif which in the course of the play will become the culminating figure of harmony, between man and woman, friend and friend, and between God and mankind: "I give them with this ring" (171).

Portia, according to Bassanio, "Doth teach . . . answers for deliverance." Let us be clear, however, about what Portia does *not* teach. The song "Tell me where is fancy bred" is not, despite rumors to the contrary, a trick to bring Bassanio, by way of the rhymes "bred . . . head . . . nourished," to the inevitable "lead." The imputation of Antonio's homosexuality is one the play can survive intact, although it may create more problems than it solves; but *this* imputation—that Portia through the most blatant trick makes her "ever virtuous and holy" father's dying inspiration nugatory—is one which, if believed, would make the rest of the play inexplicable. The idea, nicely characterized by C. L. Barber as "one of those busy-body emendations which eliminate the dramatic in seeking to elaborate it," [19] seems to have been enunciated first by J. Weiss in 1876, and has attained a depressing longevity. The New Cambridge editors approve it, and even as sophisticated a poet-critic as John Hollander says (with his bets somewhat hedged) that the song works "almost as a signal" and that it "cryptically urges the choice of the lead." [20]

As with the case of Antonio's psychosexual orientation, there is no immediate way to disprove this idea, except by appealing to our sense of the play as a whole. If Portia's

19. Barber, *Festive Comedy*, p. 174.

20. *The Untuning of the Sky* (Princeton, 1961; rpt. New York, 1970), p. 150.

father's will is to retain its aura of the numinous, and if Bassanio's fitness as Portia's lover is to be affirmed; if the casket-trial is to be one in a series of trials that includes also the trial in Venice and the trial of the rings, and if those trials are to function as dramatic metaphors for love's harmony—for which the music of this song is itself a figure: if the play is to remain a romantic comedy rather than a farce or a neatly disguised satire, then the idea that Portia tips off Bassanio has got to be dismissed. It is an idea contrary to the expectations properly aroused by the dramatic and literary conventions the play exploits: the convention, for instance, that the third trial or the third contestant will be the successful one, or even the more basic comedic convention that there is an inherent rightness in Jack's having Jill. Portia's imputed cryptic urging draws upon wholly different and irreconcilable conventions; it puts me in mind of the lady in Thurber's story who skilfully applied the conventions of one literary form in the reading of another until she had finally solved "The Macbeth Murder Mystery."

But the idea of Portia's trickery in the casket-choice cannot be passed over as a harmless aberration, since from that idea it is only a small step to the idea that Portia uses a mere trick to thwart Shylock—and the rumor of that *legal* trick is even more common than the rumor of the musical one. It is to be expected that critics who favor an ironic reading of the play should find fault with Portia's legal tactics, and that the many lawyers who have contributed to the fringe literature about the play should have pointed out any number of departures from accepted judicial procedure. But even a writer whose purpose is to "suggest . . . that [Shakespeare's] work is Christian in a way no critic can ignore," concurs in the judgment that "Portia finally wins, not with mercy, but with a legalistic trick."[21] That Portia's procedure is surprising, to Shylock and to the audience, no one

21. J. A. Bryant, Jr., *Hippolyta's View: Some Christian Aspects of Shakespeare's Plays* (Lexington, Ky., 1961), pp. 2, 41.

would deny; but the surprise we feel should not be at the exposure of judicial deceit but at the revelation of truth.

The most common charge against Portia is that she leads Shylock on. Repeatedly she affirms the "justice" of his suit ("the Venetian law / Cannot impugn you as you do proceed" [4.1.174–75]), only to turn on him at the end with the objection that "This bond doth give thee here no jot of blood" (302). And now Portia seems to have discovered some previously unmentioned laws, against shedding "one drop of Christian blood" (306) or against any alien's "direct, or indirect attempts / To seek the life of any citizen" (346–47). There have of course been many other criticisms of Portia's procedures, for instance that she seems to act simultaneously as judge and counsel for the defense, or that the suit ought to have been dismissed immediately since the flesh-bond would have been unenforceable in any court in Europe. But the more legalistic the criticism the further we are from the play's essential fictional shape and spirit.

Portia quite plainly states a part of that spirit, and an aspect of the play's parabolic significance, when she tells Shylock "as thou urgest justice, be assur'd / Thou shalt have justice more than thou desir'st" (4.1.311–12). Thus the lesson she stated earlier in discursive terms—

> That in the course of justice, none of us
> Should see salvation: we do pray for mercy,
> And the same prayer, doth teach us all to render
> The deeds of mercy—
>
> [195–98]

she now contrives to have enacted in a fully dramatic way. The spiritual truth is embodied in a secular analogue.

So much is plain. But it is also true that the artist's freedom to invent laws, judicial or otherwise, is not absolute; he does, in this matter as in all others, owe a debt to the prior creation of which he, too, is a part. Without making the literalistic error of criticizing Portia according to historical canons of law, we still must expect her legal principles to bear some similarity to those that are known in the "real" world. And in the matter of Portia's leading Shylock on—drawing out the trial rather than rendering her verdict immediately—and of seeming to discover new laws in the course of those drawn-out proceedings, there is enacted a valid legal concept. The general point is made, in the context of current American practice, by the legal scholar Harold J. Berman:

> Both 'activists' and 'conservatives' tend to treat legal rules as having an independent, objective existence; the activists would manipulate the rules to achieve desired social results, whereas the conservatives would follow the rules—both often fail to recognize that *the process of judging is a dynamic one* in which the judge (to quote Zechariah Chafee) *makes rules by finding them and finds the rules by making them.*[22]

This dynamic process of judging is what Portia is engaged in, so that the law—while still remaining the law—is made society's servant, not its master, and so that the unmitigated law before which all would stand condemned can be made to yield its mercies.

An important aspect of Portia's legal dynamic is the pedagogic function she makes the trial serve. The Venetian courtroom is the focus not only for the play's examination of justice and mercy, law and grace, works and faith; it is the focus also for its complex pattern of learning-teaching relationships. We have glanced at Portia in her dual role as pupil and teacher. Eagerly committing herself to Bassanio as "an unlesson'd girl," (3.2.159), happy to have her gentle soul "directed, / As from her lord, her governor, her king" (164–65), she is simultaneously teaching, by delighting, a lesson in social forms; and that social lesson is a model for

22. *The Interaction of Law and Religion* (Nashville, 1974), pp. 117–18; my italics.

humanity's relation to divinity itself. Portia's aptness as teacher is inseparable from her willingness to be taught, as well as from her knowledge that true discipleship is not easily achieved. With her early speech "If to do were as easy as to know what were good to do, chapels had been churches" (1.2.12 ff.), I suggested that we compare St. Paul's confession that "to wil is present with me: but I find no meanes to performe that which is good. / For I do not the good thing, which I wolde, but the evil, which I wolde not, that do I" (Rom. 7 : 18–19). From such an acknowledgement of frailty and insufficiency follows the central lesson Portia has to teach, both discursively and in action, that only through the free gift of mercy can we "see salvation."

An important clue to Portia's pedagogic function—as well as to another of the play's rings of reconciled opposites —is found in the related epithets applied to her in her role as Balthazar. The Duke says that Bellario has recommended "A young and learned doctor to our court" (4.1.144); and when the actual letter is read, again we hear " 'I never knew so young a body with so old a head' " (4.1.160–61). Shylock praises this young "Daniel come to Judgment" as a "wise young judge" (4.1.22), and again: "O wise and upright judge, / How much more elder art thou than thy looks!" (246–47). Along with these various allusions to the combination in Balthazar of youth's vigor and age's wisdom, we may recall from an earlier scene the message found by Morocco in a death's head:

> Had you been as wise as bold,
> Young in limbs, in judgment old,
> Your answer had not been inscroll'd.
>
> [2.7.70–72]

The reiterated paradoxical image, combining in one person what is best both in youth and in age, alludes to a Renaissance moral commonplace: "A man who could display his vitality with caution was called a *puer senex* or *paedogeron,* that is, a 'hoary youth.' "[23] The ideal of the *puer senex* has been traced by Ernst Curtius to origins in "late pagan Antiquity," when it was popular as a topos of praise:

> It is [Curtius continues] all the more significant, then, that the Bible had something corresponding to show. Of Tobias we read that he was the youngest of all, but never acted childishly: "Cumque esset junior omnibus . . . nihil tamen puerile gessit in opere" (1 : 4). The Wisdom of Solomon, 4 : 8 ff. declares that age is honorable but is not to be measured by years: "Wisdom is the grey hair unto men." The Vulgate has: "Cani sunt sensus hominis." The old man's grey hair, then, serves as a figurative expression for the wisdom which old age should possess. But this wisdom of old age can also be the portion of youth. . . . The topos *puer senex* was impressed on the memory of the West by a much-read text. Gregory the Great began his life of St. Benedict with the words: "Fuit vir vitae venerabilis . . . ab ipso suae pueritiae tempore cor gerens senile" ("he was a man of venerable life . . . even from his boyhood he had the understanding of an old man").[24]

The youthful Balthazar, sagely interpreting the laws—both of God and man—and slowly unravelling their difficulties until, at a stroke, the knot which had confounded the elders is severed, performs a brilliant comic *coup de théâtre;* simultaneously, and with no strain on that comic function, this figure with the young body and the wise old head performs the serious moral work, sanctioned by the best pagan and biblical models, expected of the *puer senex.*

Portia's lesson is intended for each of the principals at the trial—Shylock most directly, but also Antonio and Bas-

23. Wind, *Pagan Mysteries,* p. 99.

24. *European Literature of the Latin Middle Ages,* trans. Willard Trask (New York, 1953; rpt. 1963), pp. 99–100.

sanio. That the lesson will be wasted on Shylock is, by the time of the trial, a foregone conclusion; for just as Portia shows her aptness by confessing her weakness, so Shylock shows his incapacity by his consistently reiterated trust in the sufficiency of the law, the bond, the letter: "My deeds upon my head! I crave the law, / The penalty and forfeit of my bond" (4.1.202–03). It is almost literally the case that Shylock becomes deafer, as well as increasingly speechless, as the play proceeds. From his initial (though deceptive) expansiveness, Shylock's vocabulary becomes more limited and repetitive, as he insists monomaniacally "I'll have no speaking, I will have my bond" (3.3.17). Because he will not hear, he cannot know that the lesson he proudly declares himself proficient in is only the limited, self-defeating lesson of this world, not the truth of the spirit: "The villainy you teach me I will execute, and it shall go hard but I will better the instruction" (3.1.65–66).

Antonio, too, has been hard of hearing in the past. His response to Shylock's "Hath a dog money" speech—his shocking "I am as like to call thee so again, / To spet on thee again, to spurn thee too" (1.3.125–26)—shows how little capable, at that early point at least, Antonio is of hearing Shylock's human voice with its imperative demand for charity. In the complex of learning-teaching relationships, Antonio has indeed been guilty of teaching Shylock the false lesson of "villainy"—a fact which need not, however, lead to an exculpation of the eager pupil, Shylock. At the trial, Portia speaks of mercy to both men, but only one of them is able properly to respond.

Since the mercy Portia urges is not a matter of "compulsion" (4.1.179), Shylock dismisses its possibility entirely: "My deeds upon my head! I crave the law" (202). Refusing Bassanio's well-intentioned but misguided request that she wrest the law to her authority, Portia proceeds at Shylock's demand to fulfill every jot and tittle of the law until it yields the mercy for Antonio that Shylock would not freely grant. As for Shylock, it is consistent with what he himself has repeatedly urged that the language of compulsion is still used with him: "Down, therefore, and beg mercy of the duke" (359).

That Portia's speeches and her dramatic example have been intended for Antonio as well as for Shylock now becomes apparent. The Duke immediately gives up his legal hold over Shylock's life: "That thou shalt see the difference of our spirit / I pardon thee thy life before thou ask it" (364–65). The financial arrangements are more complicated:

> For half thy wealth, it is Antonio's,
> The other half comes to the general state,
> Which humbleness may drive unto a fine.
>
> [4.1.366–68]

In light of this official act, which charitably reduces Shylock's liability to the state from half of his wealth to a mere fine, Portia's next brief enigmatic line may at first appear a gratuitous cruelty: "Ay for the state, not for Antonio." No one, after all, has suggested that Antonio follow the Duke's example: why then must Portia appear to put a stop to an action that has not even been considered? With one further line Portia answers this question and allows Antonio—freely, of his own volition and not simply in imitation of the Duke—to show that he has learned the trial's lesson: "What mercy can you render him, Antonio?" (374). Though all the world else may remain deaf, like Gratiano with his stupid response, "A halter gratis, nothing else for Godsake!" (375), Antonio is able to amend his earlier fault. Part of the "mercy" that Antonio is able to render Shylock is unpalatable to modern sensibility, and we will have to consider this huge stumbling block of Shylock's forced conversion in the next chapter. On faith, as it were, let us here assume that Shakespeare intends no corruscating irony, but rather a demonstration of Antonio's increased harmonization, the amending in one gesture both of his own and, perforce,

Shylock's spiritual state, in his response to Portia's question. He will simply administer his half of the estate on Shylock's behalf, rendering the principal and any accruing profits to Jessica and Lorenzo at Shylock's death, provided "that for this favour / He presently become a Christian" (4.1.382–83).

4

"The Jew Shall Have All Justice" The Problem of Shylock

Launcelot Gobbo's debate between his conscience and the fiend (2.2.1–30) may be in our minds as we try to come to terms with the question of Shylock. It sometimes seems that all our conclusions on the subject must turn to "confusions" faced with the mystery of Shylock's dramatic creation. In Launcelot's debate "the fiend gives the more friendly counsel" to run from the Jew; while "conscience is but a kind of hard conscience" to bid him stay with his intractable master. The temptation to put one's heels at the fiend's commandment and run from the problem is strong.

In some ways we are better off than earlier generations, but in others worse, in the effort to see Shylock steadily and to see him whole. Behind us is the work of scholars who have given us perspective on Elizabethan attitudes toward Jews and usury, on problems of literary genetics, source-influence, conventions of characterization and dramatic construction. But behind us also is Hitler. And with us constantly are our own convictions about religion and humanity—convictions we will not lightly jettison even in the name of supposedly objective fact. Shylock bedevils the characters of the play, but he also bedevils our efforts as readers, audience, actors, or critics.

In modern times those efforts have generally taken one of two different directions—so different that their implications for the play's overall interpretation lead to the situation I mentioned in the Introduction to this book, the two-faced

Janus of the present state of critical understanding. One direction is toward Shylock's social redemption, the idea of him as a potentially good man twisted by malignant social and religious prejudice. This approach to Shylock leads, of course, to the view (to simplify it only somewhat) that *The Merchant of Venice* is a deeply ironic play about hypocritical Christians. The other direction, frequently taken in the name of historical accuracy, dismisses as mere sentimentality any efforts toward Shylock's justification. In this view *The Merchant of Venice* is a typical romantic comedy, which only by historical accident has a Jew occupying the position otherwise filled by (say) a killjoy steward.

Among Shylock's defenders two tendencies seem most significant: the sociological, which exonerates Shylock on the basis of environmental pressures, and the racial, which assimilates him to the whole appalling history of anti-Semitism. In practice the two tendencies are closely related, in spite of a potential conflict between them: the first arises from a "realistic" bias, while the latter generalizes from the particular in the manner of allegory. The sociologically-redeemed Shylock must be a figure of considerable individualism and psychological depth, capable (as he is, for instance, in Harold C. Goddard's description of him) of exhibiting those unconscious motivations produced by environmental pressures: "It is clear that he had it in him, however deep down, to be humane, kindly, and patient, and his offer to Antonio of a loan without interest seems to have been a supreme effort of this submerged Shylock to come to the surface." [1] One can disagree with details of this description—whether, say, Shylock's offer of the loan was ever intended as anything but a trap—without, however, disagreeing with what basically it implies about Shylock's mode of characterization. The discovery of "submerged" psychological depths in Shylock is testimony to the extraor-

1. Goddard, *Meaning of Shakespeare,* I : 100.

dinary degree of "felt life" that generations of critics, actors, and audiences have found in him.

The curious thing is how easily this realistic, individualizing notion of characterization can coexist with the notion that Shylock is, in the actor Henry Irving's words, the "representative of a race." Shylock proves, according to John Palmer, that Shakespeare "realised in imagination what it means to wear the star of David." [2] Of course no racial slur is intended in these formulations—though a Jew may feel that which such friends he doesn't need enemies. We can put aside for the moment our own sense of "what it means to wear the star of David" and appreciate the source, in Shakespeare's method of characterization, for this tendency to see a generalized or representative figure in Shylock. In the two tendencies I am describing we have, in effect, both the beginning and the end of Shylock's own self-defining (although theologically and morally misleading) utterance, both his "*I* am" and his "a *Jew*."

This extraordinary doubleness of characterization, which allows Shakespeare's creations to be deeply individualized while simultaneously and (at their best) without strain representative or typical, is one of the certifiable Shakespearean miracles—as well as one of the greatest difficulties for his critics. In his discursive mode the critic must separate, or even worse, choose between, modes and purposes which in Shakespeare's medium are held in easy combination. The combination—and the deceptive ease of it—can be seen even in the names he gives his characters: the same figure can be called either "Shylock" or "the Jew," "Antonio" or "the Merchant" without our feeling that the character is being called on, in the different instances, to perform different dramatic functions. The ease with which, when it is to the purpose, the generic can substitute for the personal is a distinctive mark of Shakespearean dramaturgy: Lear or

2. John Palmer, *Comic Characters of Shakespeare* (London, 1946), p. 71.

the King, Hal or the Prince, Benedick or the Married Man.

It is, as I have said, Shylock's defenders who have, even if unintentionally, most clearly shown this doubleness of characterization. Henry Irving described his great Victorian Shylock as "a representative of a race which generation after generation has been cruelly used, insulted, execrated." To him, Shylock was "the type of a persecuted race; almost the only gentleman in the play and the most ill-used." [3] But, of course, Irving's "representative" and "type" was a theatrical success precisely because he was also intensely realized and individual.

Now it was almost inevitable that the Shylock of the modern stage, being conceived at once as "the type of a persecuted race" and as an individual, should have become a "gentleman" and not a villain. The Elizabethan Shylock was also, perforce, both a type and an individual; but he was not necessarily a gentleman—any more, I will argue, then he was *necessarily* a villain. The question for us is whether Shylock's typifying function justifies exonerating him as an individual, or whether there is not at work in such exoneration a subtle kind of sentimentality. The modern stage director may eschew Victorian theatrical mannerisms and give us, in place of the larger-than-life Shylock, a Jewish businessman of dignified bearing who modestly toys with a penknife during the trial scene; but when this figure makes his final exit to the strains of the Kaddish the same question of sentimentality arises. Does Shylock earn for himself the right, within Shakespeare's play, to be associated with that magnificent prayer, or is the audience being manipulated to respond with an emotion in excess of the facts?

In Heinrich Heine's romantic vision Shylock achieved his apotheosis. Heine's treatment of him draws on both the typical and the individual in the character; but it culminates in so obviously self-indulgent a rhapsody that the en-

3. Lelyveld, *Shylock on the Stage,* pp. 83, 82.

tire process is made suspect. On the one hand, "the two chief persons of the drama are so individualized that one might swear they are not the work of a poet's fancy, but real human beings, born of woman." On the other, however, "they are more alive than the ordinary creatures that nature makes": they are immortal. Hence it is that Heine, a "wandering hunter after dreams," while touring Venice, "looked around everywhere on the Rialto to see if [he] could not find Shylock." It was the Day of Atonement, so Heine "determined to seek [his] old acquaintance in the Synagogue":

> Although I looked all around the Synagogue, I nowhere discovered the face of Shylock. And yet I felt he must be hidden under one of those white talars, praying more fervently than his fellow-believers, looking up with stormy, nay frantic wildness, to the throne of Jehovah, the hard God-King! I saw him not. But towards evening, when, according to the Jewish faith, the gates of Heaven are shut, and no prayer can then obtain admittance, I heard a voice, with a ripple of tears that were never wept by eyes. It was a sob that could only come from a breast that held in it all the martyrdom which, for eighteen centuries, had been borne by a whole tortured people. It was the death-rattle of a soul sinking down tired at heaven's gates. And I seemed to know the voice, and I felt that I had heard it long ago, when, in utter despair it moaned out, then as now, "Jessica, my girl!" [4]

This was not the only intense experience Heine had on account of *The Merchant of Venice*. He describes seeing the play at Drury Lane, where

> there stood behind me in the box a pale, fair Briton, who at the end of the Fourth Act, fell to weeping passionately, several times exclaiming, "The poor man is

4. Quoted from Variorum ed., p. 452.

> wronged!" It was a face of the noblest Grecian style, and the eyes were large and black. I have never been able to forget those large and black eyes that wept for Shylock! [5]

Modern theatergoers are discouraged from such public effusions; and critics try, in public, to keep their minds more directly on their work. But the essential emotion behind the pale, fair Briton's cry can still be heard, and coming from the most sophisticated sources. According to Graham Midgley, Shylock "is a stranger, proud of his race and its traditions, strict in his religion, sober rather than miserly in his domestic life, and filled with the idea of the sanctity of the family and family loyalty." It is dislocating to read in a modern critic this description of Shylock as Victorian paterfamilias; and equally disturbing is the fact that Midgley's Venetians would have been at home in Scott Fitzgerald's Princeton:

> Around [Shylock] is the society of Venice, a world of golden youth, richly dressed, accustomed to luxury, to feasting, to masking, of a comparatively easy virtue and of a religious outlook which, though orthodox, hardly strikes one as deep, a society faithful and courteous in its own circle and observing a formal politeness of manner and address, but quite insufferable to those outside its own circle, where Shylock is so obviously placed.[6]

What we see here is one of the chief potential difficulties with efforts to rehabilitate Shylock: not just that they may, through faults of excess, falsify Shakespeare's portrait of the Jew, but that they risk unbalancing all the rest of the play's characters as well.

Hazlitt, commenting on Kean's performance in 1814, put

5. Ibid., p. 449.

6. Graham Midgley, "*The Merchant of Venice:* A Reconsideration," *Essays in Criticism,* 10 (1960): 122–123.

the matter in a way that most succinctly shows the problem: "our sympathies are much oftener with him than with his enemies. He is honest in his vices; they are hypocrites in their virtues." [7] And this reversal of ordinary expectations, which makes "enemies" of the play's Christians and an "honest" man—or as Henry Irving thought, a "gentleman" —of the Jew, is still frequently encountered, both in and out of the theater.

The supposed "moral emptiness" of the Venetians is most resoundingly condemned by Sir Arthur Quiller-Couch (whose phrase I have just quoted) in his introduction to the New Cambridge edition. With the problematic exceptions of Antonio and Shylock, "Q" finds that "every one of the Venetian *dramatis personae* is either a 'waster' or a 'rotter' or both, and cold-hearted at that" (p. xxiii). In this scheme of the play, Antonio becomes "the indolent patron of a circle of wasters, 'born to consume the fruits of this world,' heartless, or at least unheedful, while his life lies in jeopardy through his tender, extravagantly romantic friendship for one of them" (p. xxi).

But Quiller-Couch's sense of fair play is most outraged by Jessica: "bad and disloyal, unfilial, a thief; frivolous, greedy, without any more conscience than a cat and without even a cat's redeeming love of home. Quite without heart, on worse than an animal instinct—pilfering to be carnal—she betrays her father to be a light-of-lucre carefully weighted with her sire's ducats" (p. xx). Quiller-Couch concludes this remarkable tirade by recalling (without acknowledging the source) a famous mimed episode interpolated into the play by Henry Irving: "So Shylock returns from a gay abhorrent banquet to knock on his empty and emptied house." And like Heine's pale Briton, "Q" pronounces, "Shylock is intolerably wronged" (p. xxi).

The wholesale condemnation of the lovers in a Shakespearean comedy is a remarkable situation to encounter. Not

7. Quoted in Arden ed., p. xxxiv.

even the critical hostility to Bertram in *All's Well that Ends Well* or to Proteus and Valentine in *The Two Gentlemen of Verona* approaches either the vigor or the breadth of the reaction to the Venetians. And this reaction, it should be noted, is solely against the characters and not against the play, as it tends to be with *All's Well* and *Two Gentlemen.* The critical view that condemns Salerio, Solanio, Gratiano, and Nerissa, that proclaims Bassanio a shallow fortune hunter, Antonio an infatuated homosexual, Jessica a worse than catlike cat, and Portia herself a vindictive hypocrite—that critical view simultaneously professes admiration for the play as a whole. The outraged feeling that the poor man is intolerably wronged, while it may attest to the vigor of Shakespeare's characterization, has led to the creation of a tribe of heartless fops where one had expected the cast of a romantic comedy which celebrates harmony and love, human and divine.

If an excess of sympathy for Shylock runs the danger of unbalancing the play, there is danger from the opposite extreme as well. E. E. Stoll, ever the scourge of the critical sentimentalist, is still, half a century after the publication of his *Shakespeare Studies,* the most persuasive voice from that side. Against what one senses is the special-pleading of Shylock's defenders Stoll opposes his brisk commonsense, against their wishful rhetoric his certainty of historical fact:

> Shylock was both money-lender and Jew. In him are embodied two of the deepest and most widely prevalent social antipathies of two thousand years, prevalent still, but in Shakespeare's day sanctioned by the teachings of religion besides. All that was religious in them Shakespeare probably shared like any other easy-going churchman; but all that was popular and of the people was part and parcel of his breath and blood.[8]

8. Stoll, *Shakespeare Studies* (New York, 1927; rpt. 1942), pp. 294–95.

I will have occasion to question the accuracy of Stoll's description of contemporary religious teachings. Here one should notice the rigidity of his historical determinism. If Shakespeare was "of the people," it is implied, then he could not have conceived anything that was not within the ken of that mythical lowest common denominator—leaving us to wonder again who wrote Shakespeare's plays. Surely it makes more sense to assume that Shakespeare was *not* "like any other easy-going churchman"; but rather that in matters of religion, as in matters of dramaturgy, Shakespeare was the exception, examining afresh what to less remarkable minds were the merest axioms.[9]

Stoll's treatment of the "news from Genoa" (3.1.72 ff.) is typical of his method with *The Merchant of Venice,* a method that rules out not only sentimentality but sympathy as well. If you find pathos in the loss of Shylock's ring, the turquoise he had of Leah when a bachelor (he "would not have given it for a wilderness of monkeys")—then there (according to Stoll) goes "More Elizabethan fun running to waste!" After all, "the invitation to hilarity . . . is plain and clear": "Tubul pulls the strings of a puppet already in motion. The situation is thus instinct with comedy, pathos could not possibly live in its midst" (pp. 312, 313, 315). Why not? Because "In comedy . . . things must be simple and clear-cut; a character which is to provoke laughter cannot be kept, like Buridan's ass, in equilibrium, exciting, at the

9. Cf. Wilbur Sanders, *The Dramatist and the Received Idea* (Cambridge, 1968), p. 40: "In so far as there is an Elizabethan mind, it is as much moulded by the playwrights who sought to educate its sensibility and broaden its horizons, as it moulds those playwrights. The 'orthodoxy' of a period is not an ideological steamroller that subdues all humanity to its ruling passion for the horizontal, but itself the product of the delicate, breathing organism of human society, in which cause and effect are never very sharply distinguished." Sanders' book has interesting material about attitudes toward Jews, adduced in the discussion of *The Jew of Malta;* unfortunately (since it is so challenging a book) Sanders does not discuss *MV* at any length.

same time, both sympathy and hatred. For the audience will keep its equilibrium too" (p. 319).

The equilibristic trick may not be easy, but the fact is that Shakespeare frequently demands of his audience just that sort of balancing act. There are probably as many audience laughs in *Hamlet* as in *Twelfth Night,* partly because in both plays Shakespeare exhibits "the real state of sublunary nature," in which neither emotions nor the objects which excite them have the simple definition and unity of focus demanded by Stoll. Feste's song at the end of *Twelfth Night* is an exemplary expression of Shakespeare's comic vision, which is anything *but* "simple and clear-cut." The singer's name suggests holiday, but his song—coming at the end of a play which is itself about the end of a holiday—returns us with each chorus to "every day." Its final verse balances vast stretches of time ("A great while ago the world begun") against the brevity of our mortal reach ("our play is done"). The knowledge of "play" coexists with the knowledge of striving, and then that striving itself is subsumed under the idea of pleasure: "But that's all one, our *play* is done, / And we'll *strive* to *please* you every day." And throughout, for every "hey ho" there is the answering sound of "the wind and the rain."

Stoll's no-nonsense approach was no doubt once a welcome relief from the atmosphere of misty puffery in which some Romantics had enveloped Shakespeare. If Stoll now in his turn seems old fashioned, I hope it is because we have learned that respect for historical fact need not lead, as in Stoll's method it frequently did, to esthetic impoverishment. It is useful to know that Shylock shares a dramatic kinship with Pantalone; but if we want purity of comic characterization we should stick with the *commedia dell' arte,* which knows how to keep an audience unconflicted, rather than go to Shakespeare who, on the evidence afforded by the critical responses to *The Merchant of Venice,* abounds in provocative confusions.

Neither the pale Briton's wronged Shylock nor the contentious scholar's comic villain is entirely satisfying. The episode of Leah's turquoise is a perfect case in point: neither a simple judgment for or against Shylock is adequate to it, nor will either laughter or tears—whatever difficulties this may make for actor and audience—express the range of emotional responses it legitimately demands. The brevity of the episode—Tubal tells Shylock that one of Antonio's creditors "showed me a ring that he had of your daughter for a monkey," and Shylock responds, "Out upon her!—thou torturest me Tubal,—it was my turquoise, I had it of Leah when I was a bachelor: I would not have given it for a wilderness of monkeys" (3.1.108–113)—is no argument against its complexity. The new information it gives us can not help but modify our response to Shylock. With just the fewest words Shakespeare has created a "biography" for his character: the old man we see was once a young man who courted a woman named Leah—presumably she is dead; she gave him a turquoise ring which he has treasured over the years, only now to find that the daughter born of his marriage to Leah has stolen the ring and traded it for a pet monkey. All this specificity of detail is quite unnecessary to the mere demands of the plot. And it creates difficulties. We cannot respond to a character about whom we know so much as if he were merely "a puppet on a string." These difficulties must be integrated into our sense of the play as a whole, or the episode must be rejected as a theatrical miscalculation.

The specificity of detail is especially important in its context. We have here, after all, another one of the play's various rings: not gold, like Portia's, but nonetheless valuable both intrinsically and for its symbolic associations. Shylock's cry of pain must be caused, in part at least, by something other than the monetary associations of his youthful pledge of conjugal fidelity—or why (again) has Shakespeare given us the specific knowledge of the otherwise unnecessary Leah?

Shylock's refusal ever to part willingly with Leah's ring (for I assume that "a wilderness of monkeys" is an expression of such absoluteness) seems on the face of it entirely admirable. But this little speech comes less than fifty lines after his "Hath not a Jews eyes?" speech; and the violently wrenched conclusion to that speech—its lesson of murderous revenge extracted from the assertion of common humanity—ought to put us on guard against subtly false conclusions here as well. We may hear in his "I would not have given it for a wilderness of monkeys" an ironic echo of the casket-motto, "Who chooseth me, *must give* and hazard all he hath." The immediate context of Shylock's poignant expression of fidelity, his hysterical outbursts over the loss of his ducats, certainly establishes an association between his fidelity to Leah and his less-admirable closeness in business dealings. The Shylockian proverb, "Fast bind, fast find" (2.5.53), expresses an attitude toward material wealth, but it is also entirely consonant with his attitude toward everything, including Leah's ring, that is not solely material.

Our suspicions about the "fast bind, fast find" point of view are again confirmed in act 5 when Bassanio, in the episode of Portia's ring, plays out a comic reprise of his trial before the caskets. In that culminating demonstration we see again that *giving* can be a higher virtue than keeping. Shylock's "fast bind, fast find" proverb is not so much culpable as it is limited; and its limitations can only be perceived in light of the knowledge of another system of value. That corrective system is suggested by Portia's "How far that little candle throws his beams! / So shines a good deed in a naughty world" (5.1.90–91), with its allusion to Matthew 5 : 15–16: "Nether do men light a candel, and put it vnder a bushel, but on a candelsticke, & it giueth light vnto all that are in the house. / Let your light so shine before men. . . ." Shylock's exclusive concern for thrift, closed doors, and shuttered windows is repeatedly contrasted with the outward-going love that seeks to spend itself and shine before others.

Honor, then, is due Shylock insofar as his faithfulness to his covenant with Leah suggests, as it does, the sense of obligation incurred by the Chosen People of the Old Testament covenant. But it is no accident that the portion of Scripture to which Portia alludes in her talk about brightly shining candles immediately precedes Christ's words about his relationship to that covenant: "Thinke not that I am come to destroye the Law, or the Prophetes. I am not come to destroye them, but to fulfil them." The kind of faithfulness Shylock reveals in his grief over the loss of Leah's ring is, from Shakespeare's point of view, the foundation for a higher faith; in a sense, then, the conflict in *The Merchant of Venice* is not between evil and good, but between a Good and a Better. And our response to Shylock must accommodate what is good in him. At the same time, the limited, or unfulfilled, nature of Shylock's faithfulness is made clear by comparison with an unjealous love that sees beyond the letter of the law.

Shylock's few outraged words about Leah's ring are sufficient to indicate the character's complexity, and the hazards therefore of trying to weigh in any crude scale his claims on the audience's sympathy. Simultaneously, the episode suggests the complexity of Shylock's role in the parabolic structure of the play—showing us again that in Shakespeare's mode of characterization there need not be any conflict between the demands of psychological "realism" and those of a character's representative function. It should be entirely possible to react to Shylock as a human being—that is to say, with sympathy—and also to see his treatment by Portia as proper, and to find in the harmonies of the fifth act the play's appropriate conclusion. With the idea of this characteristically Shakespearean doubleness in mind, I would like to continue the examination of Shylock. From the discussion of textual particulars there will also occasionally arise opportunities to discuss some of the historical considerations necessary for an understanding of the character: Elizabethan attitudes toward money-lending; the actual position of Jews in England; and theological matters that would have had a bearing on Shakespeare's creation of the Jew he called Shylock.

Shylock uses language as he uses money: carefully, and as a weapon. The prodigal Christians may squander their words, enjoying the luxury of rhetorical embellishment for its own sake and for the sake of the beauty it gives to life; but Shylock knows the value of a word. Not that he is a linguistic miser: he can spend as well as save. But like the proper businessman he knows the time for each, and the effectiveness of his speaking comes in large part from his canny investment in silence.[10]

His first appearance, at 1.3, is a tour de force in the use of silence to enhance speaking, and in the aggressive use of both. He dangles his few words before the impatient Bassanio, controlling him with the bait, making him leap after the words as though they were the precious ducats themselves:

> *Shylock.* Three thousand ducats, well.
> *Bassanio.* Aye sir, for three months.
> *Shylock.* For three months, well.
> *Bassanio.* For the which as I told you, Antonio shall be bound.
> *Shylock.* Antonio shall become bound, well.
> *Bassanio.* May you stead me? Will you pleasure me? Shall I know your answer?
>
> [1.3.1–7]

10. That Shylock "hoards" his words has been remarked by Leggatt, *Shakespeare's Comedy of Love*, p. 137, among others.

He allows Bassanio to seem to be in command of the scene; Bassanio must drive it forward, enumerating the items of the contract while the apparently absent-minded Shylock lags behind merely repeating them. But the absent-mindedness is part of a careful act, and he gives us sufficient indications to know who really is in control. He changes Bassanio's innocuous "Antonio shall be bound" into the more menacingly specific "shall become bound," giving two meanings to "bound," one of which is frighteningly literal. And his coolness, his unnerving ability to maintain the act in the face of Bassanio's increasing loss of self-control, tells us, through the rhetoric of silence, that we are in the presence of a master.

A lesser businessman or a lesser speaker would give way before Bassanio's "May you stead me? Will you pleasure me? Shall I know your answer?" After all, he already has Bassanio where he wants him: Bassanio's eagerness and anger betray his dependence on Shylock. But Shylock sees further profit to be made in holding him off longer:

> *Shylock.* Three thousand ducats for three months, and Antonio bound.
>
> *Bassanio.* Your answer to that.
>
> *Shylock.* Antonio is a good man.
>
> *Bassanio.* Have you heard any imputation to the contrary?
>
> *Shylock.* Ho no, no, no, no: my meaning in saying he is a good man, is to have you understand me that he is sufficient,—
>
> [1.3.8–15]

It is all so carefully built, and so daring. Shylock has invested silence and gained a misunderstanding, which immediately he converts to a pun—for Shylock, though frugal, does occasionally venture a pun, pleased to get two meanings for the price of one. A punster is not necessarily a verbal squanderer; the trick, on the contrary, is to hold fast to the precise values of a word and to demand the full rate. Here Shylock demands the mercantile meaning, "that he is sufficient," along with the moral meaning understood by Bassanio in the phrase "good man." Even the fussy, pedantic way he explains his quibble is part of the act: at the same time that he shows us the wit in what he has accomplished he warns us against dismissing it with a laugh.

Nor should it be dismissed. This splitting off of moral values from mercantile values lies at the heart of Shylock's and Antonio's mutual antipathy. Much of the rest of this scene will be an explicit debate over the practice of lending money at interest. It is this practice that most sharply distinguishes the professional methods of the play's two merchants: Antonio declares "I neither lend nor borrow / By taking nor by giving excess" (1.3.56–57); while Shylock, although he can say simply "I hate him for he is a Christian," adds to that general ground for hatred a particular one: "But more, for that in low simplicity / He lends out money gratis, and brings down / The rate of usance here with us in Venice" (35–40). From the very start, even before Shylock can haggle over the precise word to describe his kind of business (he will call "thrift" what Antonio "calls interest" [1.3.45–46]), from the moment he parcels that word "good" into separate compartments, one containing moral values and another mercantile values, he has already declared himself no harmless businessman but a usurer in the broad Elizabethan sense.

The Elizabethan horror at the idea of taking interest for the loan of money—the practice which, with little regard to the fine points of the trade, was damned under the blanket term "usury"—is not easy for us to understand, living as we do in a society where credit is the universal way. That horror was compounded of many ingredients, some deriving from the realities of a particular economic situation, others from the realm of myth or superstition, and the largest part from a shady area between the real and the imagined. The late sixteenth century, throughout Europe, was a time of rapid economic change and growth which made the necessity for credit overwhelming. But in this area, social fact and social theory were widely out of touch with each other. Writers, both ecclesiastical and lay, depending for their view of economics upon the most venerable of classical and medieval sources, were unanimous in their condemnation of the practice of "usury"—a word which emerges, as one reads the many pamphlets, sermons, even plays condemning the practice, as a sort of catch-all for every problem that seemed to be threatening the traditional fabric of society. R. H. Tawney has called usury "the mystery of iniquity in which a host of minor scandals were conveniently, if inaccurately, epitomized." [11] And the scarcely perceived divergence between the economic realities that demanded the growth of credit and the economic theory that condemned it, produced an exacerbating tension.

Antonio and Shylock refer directly to the theoretical basis for the orthodox view of money-lending: after Shylock has told the story of Jacob and his uncle Laban's sheep, Antonio asks, "is your gold and silver ewes and rams?"—to which Shylock replies, "I cannot tell, I make it breed as fast" (1.3.90–91); and later Antonio describes lending at interest as taking "a breed for barren metal" (1.3.129). The point at issue was widely known; it derived from Aristotle, and is nicely summed up by Bacon (himself a rare skeptic in the matter), "They say . . . it is against Nature, for *Money* to beget *Money*." [12] In their debate over Jacob's

11. Tawney, *Religion and the Rise of Capitalism*, p. 151.

12. To read Bacon's essay "Of Usury," with its sensible evaluation of the pros and cons of legalizing credit, and its economically-grounded decision in favor of a regulated system of lending (with different rates set for small private loans and larger commercial loans), is to realize the profound change of attitudes that was taking place at the end of this Shakespearean period. "It is better to mitigate usury by declaration," Bacon concludes, "than to suffer it to rage by connivance."

animal husbandry, Antonio and Shylock examine this proposition. As we might expect, any simple statement about what is or is not "against Nature" was likely to come under close Shakespearean scrutiny.

Before we look at that debate it should be pointed out that the bare theoretical basis would hardly have been capable of sustaining a loathing as deep and long-lasting as that of the Elizabethans for "usury." Antonio puts flesh on the theoretical skeleton when he tells Shylock:

> If thou wilt lend this money, lend it not
> As to thy friends, for when did friendship take
> A breed for barren metal of his friend?
> But lend it rather to thine enemy,
> Who if he break, thou may'st with better face
> Exact the penalty.
>
> [1.3.127–32]

Here, in the mention of "friendship," is a matter less recondite and more viscerally accessible than the Aristotelian theory that money should not "breed." And while itself irreducibly simple, the idea of "friendship" was also the cornerstone of an entire social theory, one with deep religious foundations—the social theory that elaborates Christ's injunction to love thy neighbor as thyself. In Robert Wilson's play *The Three Ladies of London* (1584), Conscience, who has just been ruined by a character called Usury, says:

> But if we should follow Gods law we should not receave
> above that wee lend.
> For if we lend for reward, how can we say we are our
> neighbors friend:
> O how blessed shall that man be that lendes without
> abuse:
> But thrice accursed shall he be that greatly covets
> us [i.e., use = usury].

The matter is not one of empty pieties, however often practice may have diverged from theory. The relation of the individual to the community (in both its secular and its religious aspects) is what finally is at stake in the condemnation of usury; and on that relationship the words of Archbishop Laud are particularly relevant: "If any man be so addicted to his private, that he neglect the common, state, he is void of the sense of piety and wisheth peace and happiness to himself in vain. For whoever he be, he must live in the body of the Commonwealth, and in the body of the church." R. H. Tawney, who quotes Laud, says of this statement: "To one holding such a creed economic individualism was hardly less abhorrent than religious nonconformity, and its repression was a not less obvious duty; for both seemed incompatible with the stability of a society in which Commonwealth and Church were one." [13]

If "usury" was universally condemned as a threat to society, the fact that the moneylender's services were nonetheless indispensable must have made the problem seem quite literally diabolical. A gesture toward an accommodation with reality was made by Parliament in 1571, when it legalized an interest rate not to exceed ten percent. The ten percent rate had in fact been set once before, by an Act of 1545, but that Act had been repealed—and *all* interest outlawed—by an Edwardian Act of 1552. The Elizabethan Act reinstated the original Act of 1545, and it did so because the abuses which arose from the total ban on taking interest proved to be much more burdensome than the legal ten percent. Still, the deep-seated prejudice against the idea of taking interest prevented passage of more comprehensive legislation which would have regulated the moneylender's increasingly complex business; hence the age was rife with cunning schemes to take wildly excessive profits. The moneylender might, for instance, be as kind as Shylock, offering to "take no doit / of usance for [his] moneys" (1.3.136–37),

13. Tawney, *Religion and the Rise of Capitalism,* p. 172.

demanding only a bond—the forfeit of which might mean total ruin for the defaulter.[14]

The Chancellor's court of equity attempted to mitigate the awful abuses caused by the common law's failure to legitimize and regulate the entire area of credit. Nonetheless the dangers of going into debt were very grave—at the same time that the necessity for going into debt was increasingly strong. And this was true at every level of society, but most spectacularly at the top. According to Lawrence Stone,

> After 1585 there was a steady deterioration in the general situation [among the peerage]. The cutting off of favours from the Crown coincided with an epidemic of gambling and high living to force a crisis in the affairs of the nobility. . . . [A]bout two-thirds of the peerage seem to have been in growing financial difficulties in the last twenty years of the reign of Elizabeth. . . . The period 1580 to 1610 in which the nobility first be-

14. The Act of 1571 essentially acknowledges the point Bacon makes in the conclusion to the essay "Of Usury" (see note 12, above). The Edwardian Act "hath not done so much good as was hoped it should, but rather the said vice of usury, and specially by the way of sales of wares and shift of interest, hath much more exceedingly abounded, to the utter undoing of many gentlemen, merchants, occupiers, and other, and to the importable hurt of the commonwealth . . . [also] there is no provision against such corrupt shifts and sales of wares, as also . . . there is no difference of pain, forfeiture or punishment upon the greater or lesser exactions and oppressions by reason of loans upon usury: Be it therefore enacted . . ." that the Act banning the taking of any interest is repealed, and the Henrician Act (which set a maximum legal rate) is revived. I quote from Joel Hurstfield and Alan G. R. Smith, eds., *Elizabethan People: State and Society* (London, 1972), pp. 67–68. Hurstfield and Smith also extract a section from Miles Mosse's *Arraignment and Conviction of Usury* (1595), one of many pamphlets attesting to the abiding moral abhorrence of interest-taking: Mosse (writing almost a quarter century after the Act quoted above) still insists that much of what is called "interest" is nonetheless really "usury." Cf., Shylock who (taking the semantic distinction still further) describes as "well-won thrift" what Antonio calls "interest" (1.3.45–46).

> came heavily dependent on credit was the one in which the dangers of borrowing—high interest rates and the potential danger of forfeiting mortgaged estates—were very real.[15]

Behind the fairy-tale atmosphere of *The Merchant of Venice,* then, can be felt the daily anxieties of an age in which "venturing" was indeed hazardous, and in which the metaphor of "a pound of flesh" might not have seemed so grotesquely foreign to actual experience.

And who in fact were the predatory moneylenders of Shakespeare's age? William Harrison, in *The Description of England* (1587), is uncommonly honest and direct when he describes "usury" as "a trade brought in by the Jews, now perfectly practiced almost by every Christian and so commonly that he is accounted but for a fool that doth lend his money for nothing." [16] Among the lower classes, money-lending continued to be what it had always been, "not a profession but a bye-employment," as Tawney puts it; "a bye-employment which is intertwined with, and often concealed by, other economic transactions. . . . In country districts the character most commonly advancing money is a yeoman, and next to him comes probably the parson." [17] In the cities, among the wealthy, money-lending was mostly carried on by "a restricted circle of great London merchants, men who first made their money in overseas or retail trading and who then turned to the money-lending business." Lawrence Stone goes on to say that

> the most favorably placed for this business were the leading mercers, silkmen, jewellers, and goldsmiths. . . . Virtually the whole of this tight little oligarchy was drawn into money-lending between 1580 and 1620. Sixteen goldsmiths and at least forty aldermen are

15. Stone, *Crisis of the Aristocracy,* pp. 542, 543–44.
16. Ed. Georges Edelen (Ithaca, N.Y., 1968), p. 203.
17. Intro. to Wilson, *Discourse Upon Usury,* pp. 21–22.

> known to have made loans to peers during this period. . . . The other two groups who were prominent in this business during these forty years—though both were of secondary importance compared with the city magnates—were lawyers and government officials.[18]

So where, among all these pillars of society, were the Shylocks and Tubals? Mostly they were in countries like Italy rather than England (which had expelled the Jews in 1290), crowded together in impoverished ghettoes. The continuing popular association of Jew and moneylender—indeed their virtual synonymity—therefore defies easy explanation. As Lawrence Stone's account makes clear, the Elizabethan moneylender was highly visible, well known to all, and unimpeachably a non-Jew. Yet everywhere in the literature of the age the equivalence of moneylender and Jew is affirmed. One reason for this bewildering state of affairs is clear: since *in theory* the business of making barren metal breed more metal was inimical to the right-minded Christian, then ipso facto the usurer must, despite the attest of eyes and ears, be Jewish!

Some small historical justification for the connection of Jew and moneylender did exist in England, although it could hardly have played as important a part in popular attitudes as did bad theology and mere prejudice. Before their expulsion from the country, the English Jews lived in an awful double bind. On the one hand, they "enjoyed" the special protection of the king—in return for which they were kept, in Cecil Roth's phrase, as "the royal milch-cow," banned from most other employment except money-lending and then freely milked of their profits by their royal patron. That patronage, and their royally induced role as moneylenders, made the Jews in turn hated by the common people, from whose violent attacks the Jewish community did indeed need the frequent protection of the king whose pro-

18. Stone, *Crisis of the Aristocracy*, pp. 532–33.

tection had made them hated in the first place. This extraordinary state of affairs was ended after the disastrous rapacity of Edward I had virtually bankrupted his Jewish communities; then, in 1290, since the Jews had lost their usefulness to him, Edward took the popular and holy course of having them expelled. England's was the first such wholesale expulsion by any European country.[19]

Suffice to sum up this excursus with the lesson that history so awfully teaches, that no imaginary compound has more power to arouse mindless passion than that of the "usurious" Jew. Therefore it should be apparent that Shakespeare has done something extraordinary in allowing Shylock to argue his case as a moneylender as well as he does. His story of the time "When Jacob graz'd his uncle Laban's sheep" (1.3.66), although presented with a purposeful obliquity, is the strongest part of that case. Jacob's biblical example (the story is drawn from Genesis 30 : 31–43) does not necessarily "make interest good," to use Antonio's contemptuous phrase (89); but it does make it more openly problematic than we might have expected. Antonio's conclusion, that the exemplum only shows how "The devil can cite Scripture for his purpose" (93), is one legitimate response; certainly there is much about Shylock's argument that should be held suspect as a sophistically false analogy.[20] But Antonio's response is not the only legitimate one.

In Shylock's treatment of it, the Old Testament pastoral interlude is made to fly directly in the face of that universally accepted Aristotelian proposition that it is "unnatural" for money to breed money. The story, in the biblical and the Shylockian version, involves some questionable eugenics,

19. Roth, *History of Jews in England,* p. 90.

20. The orthodox view of the episode in Genesis, as it is expressed in Elizabethan sermons, is given by Arnold Williams, *The Common Expositor* (Chapel Hill, 1948), pp. 170–71. It is essentially Antonio's view, which I describe below.

but the essence is simple enough: Jacob and Laban agree that for his wages Jacob will take all the newborn lambs "which were streak'd and pied" (1.3.74). (Curiously, Shylock leaves out of his account Laban's own bit of double-dealing: according to Genesis, Laban first removed from Jacob's flock all parti-colored stock, gave them to his own sons, and "set three days' journey betwixt himself and Jacob.") The resourceful Jacob peeled some of the bark off "certain wands," set them "before the fulsome ewes" while the "work of generation" was proceeding, and thus influenced the birth of "parti-colour'd lambs, and those were Jacob's." "This," Shylock concludes, "was a way to thrive, and he was blest: / And thrift is blessing if men steal it not" (1.3.71–85).

Shylock's point, of course, is that if Jacob "was blest" despite the artificial manner in which he had influenced the ostensibly "natural" process of breeding, the moneylender may similarly thrive through *his* artificial means of breeding. Antonio's response is cogent: for one thing, Jacob had been acting only as the agent of a higher power—

> This was a venture sir that Jacob serv'd for,
> A thing not in his power to bring to pass,
> But sway'd and fashion'd by the hand of heaven
> [1.3.86–88]

—and anyway, Antonio asks, "is your gold and silver ewes and rams?" (90). But Shylock's responsive shrug of the shoulders, "I cannot tell, I make it breed as fast," wittily prevents the matter from resting where Antonio confidently believes he has settled it. If Jacob's successful venture was fashioned by the hand of heaven, who is to say that Shylock's success is not under similar auspices? A phrase out of Lear's madness may be recalled in this context: "Nature's above art in that respect" (4.6.86); and, from an ostensibly more rational source, Polixenes' answer to Perdita's disdain for streaked gillyvors, that "The art itself is Nature" (*WT,* 4.4.99). Surely usury is in the province of things artful; but how could that artificial generation of money out of money take place except (*pace* Aristotle) through "an art / That Nature makes"? (*WT,* 4.4.91–92).

It is unlikely that Shylock's sly argument would have converted many of the audience from the deep-seated prejudice against the moneylender's trade. Still, it is important that Shylock gets, as it were, a fighting chance. The issue of money-lending, for those who have attended carefully to this initial exchange between the two merchants, can no longer be decided on purely abstract grounds. Shylock is allowed to open the question sufficiently so that he can be judged on the basis of what he will do in the course of the play, rather than on preconceived notions alone.

Shakespeare introduces the whole question of usury through Shylock's apparently unintentional pun on the word "good," with its separate mercantile and moral senses. It is not a particularly amusing pun: Shylock's verbal wit is generally of the plodding sort. This is true also of the next pun he ventures, when to the list of perils awaiting Antonio's argosies—"there be land-rats, and water-rats, water-thieves, and land-thieves"—he adds, "I mean pirates" (1.3. 20–21; the quarto and folio spelling, "Pyrats," makes the pun more obvious). But the wit is not intended to lie in the pun itself, but rather in the larger dramatic situation. By hiding his real verbal agility under an assumed pedantic specificity, Shylock creates the outward persona of a fussy, slow-witted old man—at the same time that he gives away the persona and shows us the glinting hard wit that goes into its creation.

That hardness appears again when, winding up his initial exchange with Bassanio, he rubs Bassanio's nose in another innocently meant word. Shylock has concluded, "I think I may take his bond," and Bassanio answers,

Be assur'd you may.
Shylock. I will be assur'd I may: and that I may be assur'd, I will bethink me,—

[1.3.24–27]

The *assurances* Shylock demands are of a different order than those gentlemanly assurances offered by Bassanio. The figure of speech Shylock uses in his neatly turned line was known to rhetoricians as *antimetabole* or, in George Puttenham's special vocabulary, "the Counterchange." Puttenham describes it as "a figure which takes a couple of words to play with in a verse, and by making them to chaunge and shift one into others place they do very pretily exchange and shift the sense." [21] In Shylock's use of it, this "pretty" exchanging of positions produces three subtle shifts of sense; not only does "assurance" move from the realm of clubby sociability to that of no-nonsense business, but even the reversed order of the repeated "will" and "may" takes up Bassanio's simple language, converting his "*be* assur'd" into the more purposefully determined "I *will* be assur'd," and his "you *may*" into a statement implying the opposite of permission: "that I *may* be assur'd, I *will* bethink me."

It is on occasions like this, especially in act 1, scene 3, when Shylock catches the Christians *au pied de la lettre,* that we see most clearly (as he intends us to see) the falseness of the assumed persona. The harmless, silly old man is there in the nervous deliberateness of his speech patterns, in his absent-mindedness (in scene 3 he several times forgets his subject, returns to it, repeats himself, introduces long-winded digressions), in his pedantic manner of explicating his own plodding witticisms. But the careful orchestration of these devices into a larger purpose is apparent even before the aside, "How like a fawning publican he looks!" (1.3.36), with its revelation of Shylock's implacable

21. Edward Arbor, ed., *The Art of English Poesy* (1589), facsimile of the 1906 rpt. (Kent State, 1970), p. 217.

refusal to "forgive" Antonio (47). The apparent meanderings return precisely to the point: despite Bassanio's impatience with Shylock's assumed slowness, it is the Christians who waste words, Shylock who puts them, like his money, to use.

Shylock continues his masterful act after the entrance of Antonio. In contrast to the decisive, brusque way in which Antonio first addresses him—

> Shylock, albeit I neither lend nor borrow
> By taking nor by giving of excess,
> Yet to supply the ripe wants of my friend,
> I'll break a custom: [*To Bassanio.*] is he yet possess'd
> How much ye would?
>
> [1.3.56–60]

—in contrast to this self-satisfied imperiousness, Shylock continues, as he has done with Bassanio, to play to the full the part of the harmless dodderer. He is outrageously absent minded, then humbly apologetic for his failing; when Antonio reminds him that the three thousand ducats are to be loaned for three months, Shylock says, "I had forgot,—three months,—" and adds with barely disguised mockery of Bassanio, "you told me so" (62). He plays with the two needy Christians, holding them off still longer:

> Well then, your bond: and let me see,—but hear you,
> Me thoughts you said, you neither lend nor borrow
> Upon advantage.
>
> [1.3.63–65]

The back-tracking change of subject, just as he is about to get to the bond, is surely calculated to madden Bassanio and Antonio; as also is his next bewildering non sequitur:

> When Jacob graz'd his uncle Laban's sheep,—
> This Jacob from our holy Abram was

> (As his wise mother wrought in his behalf)
> The third possessor: ay, he was the third.
> [1.3.66–69]

Thus, with every show of slow-witted difficulty, Shylock prepares the way for his nimble rhetoric in defense of usury.

That defense, the story of Jacob, is ended by Shylock with a typical gesture of mock self-deprecation, "I cannot tell. . . ." And again, for a moment, there appears the old man's persona, mumbling over the terms of a business deal he seems barely able to keep in mind: "Three thousand ducats, 'tis a good round sum. / Three months from twelve, then let me see the rate" (98–99). But it is only a momentary pause to set off to even greater dramatic advantage Shylock's strongest, most dazzlingly sustained speech in this scene he has so subtly dominated throughout:

> Signior Antonio, many a time and oft
> In the Rialto you have rated me
> About my moneys and my usances:
> Still have I borne it with a patient shrug,
> (For suff'rance is the badge of all our tribe);
> You call me misbeliever, cut-throat dog,
> And spet upon my Jewish gaberdine,
> And all for use of that which is mine own.
> Well then, it now appears you need my help:
> Go to then, you come to me, and you say,
> "Shylock, we would have moneys," you say so:
> You that did void your rheum upon my beard,
> And foot me as you spurn a stranger cur
> Over your threshold, moneys is your suit.
> What should I say to you? Should I not say
> "Hath a dog money? is it possible
> A cur can lend three thousand ducats?" or
> Shall I bend low, and in a bondman's key

With bated breath, and whisp'ring humbleness
Say this:
"Fair sir, you spet on me on Wednesday last,
You spurn'd me such a day, another time
You call'd me dog: and for these courtesies
I'll lend you thus much moneys"?

[1.3.101–24]

The speech has got to be quoted in its entirety: to parse it out is to lose the astonishing colloquial rhythm, the unmistakeably individualized sound of a human voice speaking, that is so much a part of its effectiveness. The tense actorly quality, as Shylock in effect imitates Antonio as well as (most remarkably) several conceivable versions of himself, is now unmistakable. Even before this speech, Shakespeare has made the role of Shylock an irresistible opportunity for any actor, who will have had to play back and forth between the surface persona and the deeper, harder character who projects it. Now, in this long speech, Shylock becomes himself an actor's actor, using his histrionic skills (as the professional actor does) simultaneously to seduce and attack his audience. This undisguised display of histrionics brings to consciousness for us one of the claims he has all along in this scene been making on our attention: we see now the intense intellectual and emotional concentration he devotes to his role-playing. We sense in Shylock the danger to which any actor is exposed, and the power he attains from that self-willed exposure. The commerce between stage and audience has kept us alert, even before we are fully conscious of what is being done; we are in a state of heightened expectation, not only about what will happen next in the "story," but about how the actor will accomplish his incredible stunt, how far he can go in his audacious playing.

The seeming paradox about Shylock's carefully turned, precisely calculated speech is that it sounds so natural, so much more vitally human than (say) Antonio's less artful directness. There is little previously in Shakespeare's career to match Shylock's virtuoso trick of seeming natural by accepting fully the necessity for role-playing. Only Richard III is Shylock's equal at the game; and though Shylock is, of course, a mere petit bourgeois in villainy compared to Richard, there are significant affinities between them. Richard's declaration of intent in *3 Henry VI,* where with delighted self-satisfaction he boasts, "Why, I can smile, and murther whiles I smile, / And cry 'Content' to that which grieves my heart, / And wet my cheek with artificial tears" (3.2.182–84), makes explicit the connection between politic villainy and a certain kind of histrionic skill. And the display of that skill, by Richard or Shylock, pleases us, even despite our moral sense, giving us a vicarious release from dull goodness by our privileged contact with a more flashily attractive, witty evil.

But no one is more pleased than the actor himself. Each is at his best when he is taking the greatest theatrical risk (the power and the danger grow together): Richard in his preposterous wooing of Lady Anne, Shylock in proposing his murderous bond "in a merry sport" (1.3.141). And while Richard openly exults, "Was ever woman in this humor woo'd? / Was ever woman in this humor won?" (*R3,* 1.2. 227–28), Shylock is more subtle about showing the pleasure he takes in his role. The very manner in which he proposes the bond is a masterpiece of self-conscious villainy; we cannot mistake it as anything other than an act, and yet we are tempted to applaud it for its sheer expertness: it outvillains villainy so far that the rarity redeems it.[22]

Shylock begins by engineering one of his menacing verbal contretemps. Of his willingness to "Supply your present wants, and take no doit / Of usance for my money," he

22. But some critics have accepted Shylock's "merry sport" at face value: H. B. Charlton, *Shakespearian Comedy* (London, 1938; rpt. 1966), p. 150; Goddard, *Meaning of Shakespeare,* 1 : 100.

concludes, "This is kind I offer" (136–38). And Bassanio, possibly with an attempt at sarcasm, replies, "This were kindness"—only to have the phrase shot back at him in a manner that converts both the "kindness" and even the innocent "this" into potential threats:

> *This kindness* will I show,
> Go with me to a notary, seal me there
> Your single bond, and (in a merry sport)
> If you repay me not on such a day
> In such a place, such sum or sums as are
> Express'd in the condition, let the forfeit
> Be nominated for an equal pound
> Of your fair flesh, to be cut off and taken
> In what part of your body pleaseth me.
> [1.3.139–147]

It is another instance of Shylock getting two meanings for the price of one. Here, he demands all the specificity of legal terminology, and at the same time manages to convey by it a disarming indefiniteness: "on such a day / In such a place, such sum or sums. . . ." He is framing an ironclad contract, already sealing off any possible escape clauses; but his language allows it to be taken as a jovial parody of legalism, another bad joke by the harmless old man. It is apparently the joke, not Shylock, that prompts the legal terminology ("forfeit," "nominated") and explicitness ("to be cut off and taken") in which the kindly offer is couched. The whole "merry" business can hardly fool the audience, which has heard in an aside of Shylock's desire to catch Antonio on the hip; and there is no evidence that it fools Antonio, who trusts not to Shylock's reasonable preference for "flesh of muttons, beefs, or goats," but to his own sufficiency: ". . . in this there can be no dismay, / My ships come home a month before the day" (1.3.176–77). But Shylock does not really intend it to deceive anyone. Rather it is a display of sheer power: Can I do this and cannot get a heart? Shylock's last fillip in the scene, "If he will take it, so,—if not, adieu, / And for my love I pray you wrong me not" (165–66), fairly drips with his contempt for the Christian fools who are so helpless before him. Although the terms of his bond seem wordy and loose, in it, as throughout the scene, Shylock magnificently proves his cunning as an investor of speech.

Shylock is as careful of his very presence as he is of his words: "I will buy with you, sell with you, talk with you, walk with you, and so following: but I will not eat with you, drink with you, nor pray with you" (1.3.30–33). And this social exclusivity is reflected in the facts of his actual dramatic career: Shylock appears in only five scenes, in one of which (3.3) he makes his exit after the seventeenth line.

The power of Shylock's stage presence, which is as manifest in the reading as it is in the role's theater history, would therefore appear to be something of a mystery. But part of that mystery can be explained, I think, by the memory we carry throughout the play of Shylock's histrionic mastery in scene three, as that memory is then played off against the reality of Shylock's successive degeneration. Rhetorical tricks, especially his feigned absent-mindedness and contrived repetitions, which in his first appearance were aspects of his dominance, become in later scenes a product of the man himself, not of his persona; they become signs of weakness rather than of strength. And the contrast itself is arresting.

Flashes of the original Shylock, whose witty performance had engaged our attention despite our moral scruples, remain almost to the end of the trial scene. But increasingly those remnants of beleaguered cunning serve only to throw into relief other moments when he loses his tense self-control—at home, for instance, wearily with Jessica:

> I am bid forth to supper Jessica,
> There are my keys:—but wherefore should I go?
> I am not bid for love. . . .
>
> [2.5.11–13]

—or in the stuttering rage of "You knew, none so well, none so well as you, of my daughter's flight" (3.1.22–23). Commenting on Macklin's performance in 1775, Georg Lichtenberg gave this description which catches exactly the effect of contrast I am interested in:

> The first words he utters, when he comes on to the stage, are slowly and impressively spoken. . . . Three such words uttered thus at the outset give the keynote of his whole character. In the scene where he first misses his daughter, he comes on hatless, with disordered hair, some locks a finger long standing on end, as if raised by a breath of wind from the gallows, so distracted was his demeanoùr. Both his hands are clenched, and his movements abrupt and convulsive. To see a deceiver, who is usually calm and resolute, in such a state of agitation, is terrible.[23]

The fright-wig and some of the accompanying business may be altered to suit contemporary taste, but Lichtenberg's concluding phrase—"To see a deceiver, who is usually calm and resolute, in such a state of agitation, is terrible"—ought to describe our response to any adequate performance of the role.

Act 1, scene 3—the scene in which Shylock establishes his strength—is, of course, an entirely "public" scene, between Shylock and the Christians, with Shylock at every point tensely alert. His next appearance (2.5)—which follows immediately upon our learning, from Lorenzo, of Jessica's

23. Quoted in John Russell Brown, "The Realization of Shylock: a Theatrical Criticism," *Early Shakespeare,* Stratford-upon-Avon Studies, 3 (London, 1961): 190.

intended elopement—is a "private" scene: Shylock with Launcelot and Jessica, concerning himself with domestic affairs, preparing to go forth to supper. And the effect, therefore, is complex. A relatively more relaxed Shylock is here "humanized"; that, and our knowledge of the real "ill a-brewing to [his] rest," engages our sympathy for him. But by the same token, signs of weakness that are beginning to emerge in Shylock qualify the impression we have carried over from his first appearance. And to the extent that his witty performance in that earlier scene has earned our complicity with him, these hints at his degeneration will make us feel cheated, make us question whether we have not indeed been seduced into taking the fool's gold of flashy evil when we should have known from the start the greater desirability of pale and leaden goodness.

The "witty" Shylock is still apparent in the way he converts an invitation to dine *with* Antonio into an occasion "to *feed upon* / The prodigal Christian" (2.5.14–15). But the cannibalistic menace flashes only briefly out of a more pervasive sense of weariness. Losing his train of thought and repeating himself are no longer tactics to tantalize the listener but an unconscious habit:

> I am bid forth to supper Jessica,
> There are my keys:—but wherefore should I go?
> I am not bid for love, they flatter me,
> But yet I'll go in hate, to feed upon
> The prodigal Christian. Jessica my girl,
> Look to my house,—I am right loath to go,
> There is some ill a-brewing to my rest,
> For I did dream of money-bags to-night.
>
> [2.5.11–18]

Even that sharp declension from the idea of dining with someone for love into feeding on someone in hate is undercut by Shylock's petty concern to make the "prodigal Christian" "waste / his borrowed purse" (49–50). There is at once something touching about Shylock's attitude towards the defecting Launcelot ("The patch is kind enough") and faintly ridiculous ("but a huge feeder" [45]). The economic advantage from which Shylock derived his confidence in his first appearance degenerates in this scene into the obsessions of the mere miser. The stinginess, which in his first scene he displayed even in his brilliantly sparing use of language, is now ridiculously extended to include a distaste for music and merriment:

> What are there masques? Hear you me Jessica,
> Lock up my doors, and when you hear the drum
> And the vile squealing of the wry-neck'd fife
> Clamber not you up to the casements then
> Nor thrust your head into the public street
> To gaze on Christian fools with varnish'd faces:
> But stop my house's ears, I mean my casements,
> Let not the sound of shallow fopp'ry enter
> My sober house.
>
> [2.5.28–36]

The pedantic explication of a plodding joke—"my house's ears, I mean my casements"—now has no histrionic justification; it remains a pedantic explication of a plodding joke. Shylock's final words in this scene, "Fast bind, fast find,— / A proverb never stale in thrifty mind," *are* stale. Compared to the way he took his exit several scenes earlier, we are left with the image now of a sadly diminished figure. We can sympathize with that figure, but we can also see him more clearly for what he is.

Shylock's next appearance is in act 3, scene 1: it is the extraordinary scene which includes Shylock's "Hath not a Jew eyes" speech, with its perverse conclusion in Shylock's flaunting his superiority in villainy, and the news of Leah's turquoise ring. The rapid changes of mood as Shylock responds to Tubal's news—exulting at Antonio's losses, bemoaning his own—has no doubt its comic aspect, although "absurd" might be a better word if it more readily comprehends other effects produced by the scene. For this is the scene to which Lichtenberg referred when he described the "terrible" effect of Shylock's degeneration from the character as he appeared in act 1, scene 3.

Shakespeare cannily holds off Shylock's entrance until we have had some typically urbane, easy, and cheap talk from Solanio and Salerio. Their shallow concern for Antonio ("it is true, without any slips of prolixity, or crossing the plain highway of talk, that the good Antonio, the honest Antonio;—O that I had a title good enough to keep his name company!—" [3.1.10–14]) is the perfect foil to set off the dazed fury of Shylock's entrance. And their continued baiting of him—driving him, incidentally, to that greatest if most rhetorically deceitful speech of all, "Hath not a Jew eyes"—makes of Shylock's sudden repeated reversals of emotion with Tubal an image of our own complex feelings about him. The laughter is strangled by horror—at what is done to him, but also at what he himself is doing; and at what menacing but also ridiculously petty thing he has conspired with his enemies to make of himself: "I will have the heart of him if he forfeit, for were he out of Venice I can make what merchandise I will" (116–18).

Only one scene separates Shylock's appearance here from his next appearance (3.3). The intervening scene is the one in which Bassanio undergoes the casket trial and wins Portia, in which news comes of Antonio's utter failure to "scape the dreadful touch / Of merchant-marring rocks" (3.2.269–70), and in which Portia grandly offers "To pay the petty debt twenty times over" (306):

> Pay him six thousand, and deface the bond:
> Double six thousand, and then treble that,
> Before a friend of this description
> Shall lose a hair through Bassanio's fault.
>
> [3.2.298–301]

It is in every way an expansive scene, of great expectations expressed in heroic mythical allusions (Portia calls Bassanio the "young Alcides," a "Hercules" [55, 60]; and when he has succeeded at the trial he says, "We are the Jasons, we have won the fleece" [240]); there is music in the scene and rich metaphor and the actual language of multiplication: "I would be trebled twenty times myself, / A thousand times more fair, ten thousand times more rich" (153–54). Like Portia herself, everything about the scene seems striving to "exceed account" (157). And no contrast in the play is more stark than the contrast between this long scene of outward-flowing richness and the short scene following it, which begins with Shylock's, "Gaoler, look to him."

In the seventeen lines before Shylock makes his exit from act 3, scene 3 he reaches his moral, and simultaneously his linguistic, nadir. The technique of verbal repetition, which had once been a source of flexibility for Shylock, is here the enacted symbol of his own imprisonment within the self-defeating system of vengeance. To speak well was, for the Renaissance, the very proof of humanity, the ability that separates man from beast. A textbook of logic (Thomas Wilson's *Rule of Reason* [1551]) gives as its example of "an undoubted true proposition" the definition, "A man is a liuing creature endewed with reason, hauing aptnesse by nature to speake." Sir Philip Sidney expresses the commonplace association, "*Oratio* next to *Ratio,* Speech next to Reason, [is] the greatest gift bestowed vpon mortalitie." [24] Shylock's speech is now reduced to the obsessive repetition of phrases connoting restriction; simultaneously he refuses

24. *An Apologie for Poetrie,* in *Elizabethan Critical Essays,* ed. G. Gregory Smith (Oxford, 1904), 1 : 182. Cf., Ben Jonson: "*Speech* is the only benefit man hath to express his excellency of mind above other creatures. It is the instrument of *Society.*" (*Timber, or Discoveries,* in *Ben Jonson's Literary Criticism,* ed. James D. Redwine, Jr. [Lincoln, Nebraska, 1970], p. 20.) See also Lawrence Danson, *Tragic Alphabet: Shakespeare's Drama of Language* (New Haven, 1974), pp. 2–7.

others the freedom of speaking, revealing himself as one who, although undoubtedly sinned against, has of his own free will given up the outward sign of humanity. Thus his threat, "Thou call'dst me dog before thou hadst a cause, / But since I am a dog, beware my fangs" (3.3.6–7), has an almost literal as well as figurative truth:

> *Shylock.* Gaoler, look to him—tell not me of mercy,—
> This is the fool that lent out money gratis.
> Gaoler, look to him.
> *Antonio.* Hear me yet good Shylock.
> *Shylock.* I'll have my bond, speak not against my bond,—
> I have sworn an oath, that I will have my bond:
> Thou call'dst me dog before thou hadst a cause,
> But since I am a dog, beware my fangs,—
> The duke shall grant me justice,—I do wonder
> (Thou naughty gaoler) that thou art so fond
> To come abroad with him at his request.
> *Antonio.* I pray thee hear me speak.
> *Shylock.* I'll have my bond. I will not hear thee speak,
> I'll have my bond, and therefore speak no more.
> I'll not be made a soft and dull-ey'd fool,
> To shake the head, relent, and sigh, and yield
> To Christian intercessors: follow not,—
> I'll have no more speaking, I will have my bond.
> [*Exit*] [3.3.1–17]

The linguistic degeneration displayed here is the ironically appropriate fate of the diabolical literalist.

Shylock has only one more scene in the play: the trial. And there too, of course, his unreasonable and uncharitable literalism is self-defeating. Shylock himself has established the apparent absoluteness of the alternatives in that trial: "tell not me of mercy. . . . the duke shall grant me justice." And it is that sense of absoluteness that makes Portia's procedure so remarkable (approaching, as I have suggested, the realm of miracle), showing harmony where there had appeared to be only unalterable division.

A merciful justice is extended to Shylock as well as to Antonio, and Shylock too is accommodated within the final harmony. But these are matters not easily accepted by a modern audience, and deserve further attention. Certainly there would be a moral obtuseness displayed by any modern audience not made at least queasy by the financial penalties imposed on Shylock and—the greatest stumbling block—by his forced conversion. But setting these matters in the context of Shakespeare's comic and Christian vision may at least make them understandable.

Antonio's free decision to administer his half of the estate on Shylock's behalf, with the proviso that at Shylock's death all of it will go to Jessica and Lorenzo, would have seemed more generous to an Elizabethan audience than it does to us, considering the Elizabethan abhorrence of usury. As a moneylender, all Shylock's wealth has supposedly been ill-gained; its total confiscation would not have seemed an unduly severe penalty. It is conceivable, even, that some of Shakespeare's audience were aware of historical precedent for the confiscation of a convert's wealth. For there still existed into the early seventeenth century, although in a state of decline, a curious institution in London called the *Domus Conversorum,* a hostel for Jewish converts that had originally been established in 1232. According to Cecil Roth, the *Domus Conversorum* was set up because, "Legally, converts from Judaism forfeited to the Crown all their property, as having been acquired by the sinful means of usury. Destitute as they were, a hostel was indispensable" (p. 43). The absurdity of the medieval situation—the encouraging (to put it mildly) of conversion, the subsequent reward for which was to be made an impoverished ward of the state—led to a modification of the law in 1280. The king at that time "waived for a seven-year period his legal claim on the property of those who left their faith. From now on they might retain one-half of what they previously owned, though amassed in sin, the remainder (with certain other income from Jewry, including the proceeds of the recently instituted poll tax) being devoted to the upkeep of the *Domus Conversorum* in London."[25]

So there was historical precedent in England both for the confiscation of the convert's property and for the remission of one-half of that penalty. There was historical precedent for enforced conversion as well; but in this matter we must look to biblical salvation-history as well as to the history of nations. I have said that Shylock's unyieldingness suggests, even if in a perverted form, the Old Testament covenant. But the Jew had another claim on the Christian, one which was in fact to contribute to the eventual recall of the Jews to England in 1655. That claim is the Jew's unique and necessary position in the scheme of man's salvation.

In Isaiah it is prophesied that "The remnant shall returne, *euen* the remnant of Iaakob vnto the mighty God" (10 : 21). And the return of that saving remnant—the conversion of the Jews—must occur before all things can be

25. Roth, *History of Jews in England,* p. 79. Among the observations made by that fantastical traveler, Thomas Coryat, in his visit to the Venetian ghetto in the first decade of the seventeenth century is this: "And as pitiful it is to see that fewe of them [i.e., the Jews] living in Italy are converted to the Christian religion. For this I understand is the maine impediment to their conversion: All their goodes are confiscated as soone as they embrace Christianity: and this I heard is the reason, because whereas many of them doe raise their fortunes by usury . . . it is therefore decreed by the Pope, and other free Princes in whose territories they live, that they shall make restitution of their ill gotten goods, and so disclogge their soules and consciences, when they are admitted by holy baptisme into the bosome of Christs Church. Seeing then when their goods are taken from them at their conversion, they are left even naked, and destitute of their meanes of maintenance, there are fewer Jewes converted to Christianity in Italy, than in any other country of Christendome." *Coryat's Crudities* (1611) (Glasgow, 1905), 1 : 373–74.

accomplished and God's Kingdom be established.[26] In Romans, St. Paul elaborates on Isaiah's prophecy and on the role of the Jews in salvation-history. The question he is addressing for the benefit of his Gentile audience is whether the calling of the Gentiles has entailed the rejection of the Jews; his answer is one of his most elaborate "God forbids!" Paul cites Isaiah 65 : 2, "And vnto Israel he saith, All the day long haue I stretched forthe mine hand vnto a disobedient, and gainsaying people" (Rom. 10 : 21). God has not rejected the Jews; it is the Jews, rather, who have put their trust in "the workes of the Law" rather than seeking salvation by faith (Rom. 9 : 32): "According as it is written, God hathe giuen them the spirit of slomber: eyes that they shulde not se, & eares that they shulde not heare vnto this day" (Rom. 11 : 8). Because of this deafness, the Law itself has become, as David prophesied, "a snare, & a net, & a stombling blocke" (11.9)—a verse glossed in the Geneva Bible as follows: "Christ by the mouth of the Prophet wisheth that which came upon the Iewes, that is, that as birdes are taken where as they thinke to finde fode, so the Law which the Iewes of a blinde zeale preferred to the Gospel thinking to haue saluation by it, shulde turne to their destruction."

It is not Portia but Shylock himself, in his "blinde zeale" demanding the law, his deeds upon his head, who makes the law "a snare, & a net, & a stombling blocke." Shylock demands it, and Portia gives it: "The Jew shall have all justice" (4.1.317). Bringing destruction upon himself through a vain self-righteousness, and failing to hear

26. Cf. Harold Fisch, *The Dual Image: The Figure of the Jew in English and American Literature* (New York, 1971), pp. 14–15: "The Jews [according to traditions based on Pauline doctrine] were a deicide nation but they were also a nation which is redeemed, and on whose redemption the fate of mankind hangs." See also an interesting article by Albert Wertheim, "The Treatment of Shylock and Thematic Integrity in *The Merchant of Venice*," *Shakespeare Studies*, 6 (1970) : 75–87. See also G. K. Hunter's "The Theology of *The Jew of Malta*," *op. cit.*

the Gospel message of mercy freely granted, Shylock at his trial plays out the role of the Jew as it appears in the New Testament version of salvation-history.

That role has a further dimension, a dimension suggested by Shylock's conversion and by the subsequent comic joys of act 5. In St. Paul's version of Jewish history, the falling off of God's Chosen People is one in a series of "fortunate falls," each preparing the way for a greater joy to come. The "obstinacie"—or as the Authorized Version calls it, the "blindness"—of the Jews has come upon them "vntil the fulnes of the Gentiles be come in" (Rom. 11 : 25). This "secret" Paul imparts to the Gentiles "lest ye shulde be arrogant in your selues," reminding them that "all Israel shalbe saued, as it is written, The deliuerer shal come out of Sion, and shal turne away the vngodlines from Iacob" (25–26). Therefore, says Paul, the Jews of the present day have a complex relationship to the newly-chosen Christians: "As concerning the Gospel, they are enemies for your sakes: but as touching the election, they are beloued for the fathers sakes" (Rom. 11 : 28).

And all the more to be beloved for the role Israel plays in God's scheme of "fortunate falls":

> For euen as ye in time past haue not beleued God, yet haue now obteined mercie through their vnbelefe, / Euen so now haue they not beleued by the mercie shewed vnto you, that they may also obteine mercie. / For God hathe shut vp all in vnbelefe, that he might haue mercie on all. [Rom. 11 : 30–32]

Thus salvation was made possible for the believing Gentiles through the unbelief of Israel; and now Israel's unbelief will allow God to show his free mercy to the Jews when in time their unbelief shall pass away. As Adam's disobedience was made the occasion for God's mercy to Adam's descendants, so the Jews, when they have acknowledged the insufficiency of their "blinde zeale" to the law, will discover the mystery of grace. The casting away of the Jews was the reconciling of the rest of the world; and their eventual reception shall be life from the dead for all (Rom. 11 : 15). As the glossator of the Geneva Bible writes: "The Iewes now remaine, as it were, in death for lacke of the Gospel: but when bothe they & the Gentiles shal embrace Christ, the world shalbe restored to a new life."

In the medieval cycle plays or a miracle play like *The Croxton Play of the Sacrament,* where present time is regarded *sub specie aeternitatis,* a converted Jew could recognize his glorious culminating place in history and rejoice accordingly. Shakespeare's drama, however, while it affords intimations of the Last Things, accepts stricter limits; it shows mankind, however beautifully arrayed, still wearing its muddy vestures of decay. Thus Shylock's response to the court's merciful extortion of his wealth and his religion is the brief, "I am content"—which may be pronounced bitterly or, as I believe it should be, with a profound weariness, the final stage in that successive weakening we have observed in him since his first bold appearance; followed by his anticlimactic exit lines:

> I pray you give me leave to go from hence,
> I am not well—send the deed after me,
> And I will sign it.
>
> [4.1.391–93]

How to react to these proceedings? Gratiano's capering vindictiveness—

> In christ'ning shalt thou have two godfathers,—
> Had I been judge, thou shouldst have ten more,
> To bring thee to the gallows, not to the font
>
> [4.1.394–96]

—is certainly *not* intended as the final commentary. Rather, the final commentary is conveyed more lengthily and obliquely, by all that follows in the play. As the nightmarishly bright light of the courtroom recedes and we awaken into the candlelit peace of Belmont, those whose "spirits are attentive" will hear a "concord of sweet sounds" which, entering into the heart, may give a promise beyond all this world's discords of the "harmony . . . in immortal souls."

5

"Touches of Sweet Harmony" Fulfillment and Reconciliation in *The Merchant of Venice*

There are heard melodies in *The Merchant of Venice:* the song "Tell me where is Fancy bred" accompanies Bassanio's casket-choice, and in act 5 Lorenzo calls upon Portia's musicians to "draw her home with music" (1.70). There are unheard melodies too. A masque had been planned in Venice. It should have been accompanied by fife and drum, and against its "sound of shallow fopp'ry" Shylock had warned Jessica to "stop my house's ears" (2.5.29–36). But that joyfully raucous noise had to be postponed in favor of the more serious business of wooing. Now, in act 5, a sweeter sort of unheard melody is invoked by Lorenzo for the benefit of the attentive Jessica; the heard music that sounds throughout much of the last act is a sensory approximation of that heavenly music which (as Lorenzo explains) sounds just beyond the threshold of our gross mortal perceptions.

The limits of sensory experience and the folly of trusting to even the most reasonable shows of the world are alluded to several times in the play. It is a part of the "moral" of the casket-trials. Those who "choose by show" (2.9.26), taking their evidence only from what can be seen or heard, will never choose aright. Those "worldly choosers" are contrasted with another sort who "choose not by the view" (3.2.131); the latter enact a secular demonstration of the faith which, according to St. Paul, "is the grounde of things, which are hoped for, and the euidence of things which are not sene" (Heb. 11 : 1). At one extreme stands Shylock, whose faithful adherence to the literal makes him deaf and blind to what might be discovered in "soft stillness and the night" (5.1.56). But in Belmont, in the last act, the person who has an attentive ear and a spiritual eye is granted a fleeting perception, muted and lit only by candle and stars, of "the deepe things of God" (1 Cor. 2 : 10).

The "song . . . the whilst Bassanio comments on the caskets to himself" (3.2.62 s.d.) alludes to this distinction between the different modes and objects of perception:

> Tell me where is Fancy bred?
> Or in the heart, or in the head?
> How begot, how nourished?
> *All.* Reply, reply.
> It is engend'red in the eyes,
> With gazing fed, and Fancy dies
> In the cradle where it lies:
> Let us all ring Fancy's knell.
> I'll begin it. Ding, dong, bell.
>
> [3.2.63–71]

This brief history of the infant death of Fancy, the doomed child of the eyes, provides only a partial "reply" to the questions it poses. "Fancy," we learn, is not bred in either heart or head; but what *is* born and nourished in those more suitable nurseries? The answer, of course, is true love, an emotion or state of knowledge, like St. Paul's faith in things unseen, which has little to do with "outward shows" (3.2.73). The eyes have no sufficiently nutritive food for their fanciful progeny; moreover the "ornament" that attracts the eyes

> is but the guiled shore
> To a most dangerous sea: the beauteous scarf
> Veiling an Indian beauty; in a word,

The seeming truth which cunning times put on
To entrap the wisest.

[3.2.97–101]

And the wiser one is, therefore, in the shows of the world, and the keener one's eye for deceptive "ornament," the more one is in danger of running upon the "merchant-marring rocks" of the world's "most dangerous sea." "For ye wisdome of this worlde is foolishnes with God" (1 Cor. 3 : 19).

When Bassanio chooses the "meagre lead" whose "paleness moves [him] more than eloquence" (3.2.104, 106), he finds within the casket "Fair Portia's counterfeit" (115). The portrait's beauty astonishes him, and his description of the painter's art has strangely ominous overtones in the moment of triumph:

here in her hairs
The painter plays the spider, and hath woven
A golden mesh t'entrap the hearts of men
Faster than gnats in cobwebs,—but her eyes!
How could he see to do them? having made one,
Methinks it should have power to steal both his
And leave itself unfurnish'd.

[3.2.120–26]

The breathless praise is disturbingly conventional, and the talk of entrapped hearts and stolen eyes harks back to the mode of those who "choose by show." At this crucial instant, Portia's beauty, woven in "a golden mesh" by the spidery artist, is all-too-literally captivating. Bassanio's perception is momentarily that of the eye-engendered worldly-wise "Fancy" and, unwittingly, it turns the "counterfeit" Portia into a Circe-figure, a *belle dame sans merci* whose feeding famishes those who hunger for her most.

But Fancy is indeed evanescent, and Bassanio quickly recovers his sense of proportion. His hyperbolic and ominous praise has underprized "this shadow"—her portrait—by gilding it with the fool's gold of deceiving rhetoric; but by even more, Bassanio says, the shadowy portrait "Doth limp behind the substance" (128–29). And so from beauty's ensnaring shadow he turns to the substance, the veritable breathing Portia; and in language that begins to exorcise and redeem the play's language of law, of business, of bonds and bondage, he tells her "I come by note to give, and to receive" the prize of mutual love.

Still Bassanio has not quite passed the treacherous straits that lead to his goal. And the perils in the way are still spoken of in terms of perception, especially that of the eye. His following simile describes a kind of derangement of the senses: the hearing insufficiently discriminating, eyesight unfocused; the spirit giddy, the gaze doubtful:

> Like one of two contending in a prize
> That thinks he hath done well in people's eyes,
> Hearing applause and universal shout,
> Giddy in spirit, still gazing in a doubt
> Whether those peals of praise be his or no,
> So (thrice-fair lady) stand I even so,
> As doubtful whether what I see be true,
> Until confirm'd, sign'd, ratified by you.
>
> [3.2.141–48]

But Portia's confirmation, her bond of love, affirms in language appropriately stark—purged of rhyme and all other "ornament" that might "scarf" the truth—that she and Bassanio now see face to face: "You see me Lord Bassanio where I stand, / Such as I am" (149–50).[1]

Outward shows can be deceiving and the eye, especially, is an untrustworthy organ: the thing to notice about the idea is not its commonness but the astonishing number of changes Shakespeare worked on his persistent concern. The deceptiveness of worldly seeing is the substance of Glouces-

1. See the interesting comments by Leggatt, *Comedy of Love,* p. 134.

ter's tragedy, who stumbled when he saw; it is the pity of Othello, who demanded ocular proof of Desdemona's stolen hours of lust. With most horrible irony, Leontes thinks himself accursed for having a "true opinion" and wishes for "lesser knowledge" than what his sight has given him:

> There may be in the cup
> A spider steep'd, and one may drink; depart,
> And yet partake no venom (for his knowledge
> Is not infected), but if one present
> Th'abhorr'd ingredient to his eye, make known
> How he hath drunk, he cracks his gorge, his sides,
> With violent hefts. I have drunk, and seen the
> spider.
>
> [*WT*, 2.1.36–45]

What in fact he has seen is his friend recalling for Hermione the innocent joys of their unfallen youth; and even as Polixenes recreates through his words that time when they might have answered heaven boldly, "Not guilty," Leontes gives himself over to the deceptive evidence of the senses and violently sins against the spirit of love. To repair the sensual fault, "It is requir'd," as Paulina directs, "You do awake your faith" (5.3.94–95).

One of the most pertinent variations on the theme occurs in the Claudio-Hero plot of *Much Ado About Nothing*. The villainous Don John's method is to create, Iago-like, "such seeming truth of Hero's disloyalty, that jealousy shall be call'd assurance" (2.2.48–49).[2] His challenge to Claudio, who will be made to see a counterfeit Hero seeming to be disloyal, emphasizes the different ways of seeing and knowing: "If you dare not trust that you see, confess not that you know" (3.2.119–20). The proposition appears self-evident: what enters through the material eye must be known and trusted. But the false knowledge engendered in Claudio's

2. Cf., the line from *MV:* "The seeming truth which cunning times put on" (3.2.100).

eye creates the ensuing terrible muddle; and it is left to Dogberry's inept watch to unravel the confusion of those eminently reasonable men, Claudio and Don Pedro. Shakespeare allows Borachio, of all people, to draw the proper conclusion: "I have deceiv'd even your very eyes. What your wisdoms could not discover, these shallow fools have brought to light . . ." (5.1.232–34). Chastened now, and willing to become a fool that he may be wise, Claudio agrees to take, literally sight unseen, the proposed substitute bride. But when the veil is lifted there appears "The former Hero! Hero that is dead!" (5.4.65). There is, of course, a simple enough explanation for this apparently miraculous restoration; but the Friar, withholding that explanation from Claudio until the "holy rites" have been completed, directs both the characters and the audience in the appropriate response: "Mean time let wonder seem familiar" (5.4.70.)

"The moon shines bright": four gentle stage-setting syllables at the opening of the final act of *The Merchant of Venice* distance us from the dangerous courtroom and begin to prepare us for the "touches of sweet harmony" that can be heard in Belmont's night. The following love-duet between Jessica and Lorenzo, in which they remember less fortunate lovers who once watched "in such a night as this," is all the more charming for the playful, teasing note that threads its way through it. One function of the lovers' sophisticated exchange is, in effect, to make—for the audience and for Jessica, the gentle newcomer—"wonder seem familiar."

Lorenzo begins with a beautifully sustained but emotionally ambiguous comparison. This night of lovers' meeting is like one in which "the sweet wind did gently kiss the trees" (5.1.2), and the trees, allowing nature's soft love-play, "did make no noise." "In such a night" Troilus, at one with the mood of the time, "mounted the Trojan walls," and like the gently kissing wind he "sigh'd." But here Lorenzo's description acknowledges the harsh fact of the myth we already know, that Troilus "sigh'd his soul toward the Grecian tents / Where Cressid lay that night." The name of Cressida, because of what we know of its infamous owner and even because of the jarring sound of its initial consonants, makes of what now is called *"that* night" a night of ill-omen. The complex movement, with its subtle hesitations and repetitions, from Lorenzo's first "In such a night as this" through the medial "in such a night" to his concluding "that night," is ambiguously seductive, simultaneously attractive and dangerous.

Jessica answers Lorenzo's "In such a night" with one of her own, when "Thisbe fearfully [o'ertripped] the dew, / And saw the lion's shadow ere himself, / And ran dismayed away" (5.1.7–9). And so their exchange continues, through a catalogue of love's evils and dangers as they are figured in the stories of Cressida, Thisbe, Dido, Medea. And Jessica and Lorenzo? The rhetorical forward momentum *almost* forces the lovers of "this night" into the tragic realm implicit in the other "legends of good women." [3] But it is precisely the movement out of legend into the realm of living flesh and blood that averts the tragic:

Lorenzo. In such a night
Did Jessica steal from the wealthy Jew,
And with an unthrift love did run from Venice,
As far as Belmont.
Jessica. In such a night
Did young Lorenzo swear he loved her well,
Stealing her soul with many vows of faith,
And ne'er a true one.
Lorenzo. In such a night

3. Brown, Arden ed., notes: "Hunter [in *New Illustrations* (1845)] . . . detailed Shakespeare's debt to Chaucer and Ovid. He suggested that a folio edition of Chaucer was lying open before him, for there he would find Thisbe, Dido, and Medea in *The Legend of Good Women,* immediately preceded by *Troilus."*

Did pretty Jessica (like a little shrew)
Slander her love, and he forgave it her.
Jessica. I would out-night you did nobody come:
But hark, I hear the footing of a man.

[5.1.14–24]

The lovers' mock-combat is broken off, not by the disasters of tragedy, but by the arrival of Portia's harbinger. Most importantly, it is broken off only when the artificial world of mythical lovers has melted into this present night when Jessica and Lorenzo, confident in each other's love, can convert the language of shrewishness and slander into the word of forgiveness.

For many critics of the play, Jessica and Lorenzo have seemed sorely in need of forgiveness; the lovers seem to have much to answer for. Indeed Shakespeare allows Lorenzo himself to allude to the supposed wrongdoings: Jessica in fact "did . . . steal from the wealthy Jew"; and the squandering of Leah's ring might indeed seem to convict her of "an unthrift love." The business of Jessica and Lorenzo needs looking into, especially since, in the play's next exquisite movement, it will be this pair of lovers who speak about that music of the spheres which the play's other harmonies imitate.

Lorenzo's syntax leaves it unclear whether Jessica's "unthrift love" refers to a quality possessed by her or to Lorenzo himself, the "unthrift love" with whom she "did run from Venice." It could be either, or both; but in any case it must be understood—although the teasingly ironic, sophisticated mode of their lovers' exchange makes it possible to misconstrue the matter—as a compliment, not a condemnation. It is, after all, Shylock's "thrifty mind" that considers "Fast bind, fast find" to be "a proverb never stale" (2.5.53–54). And it is against the standard of Shylock's self-enclosing thriftiness that the lovers'—including especially his daughter's—"unthrift love" should be measured.[4]

4. Cf., Brown, "Love's Wealth," in his *Shakespeare and His Comedies.*

Although he has remained until now a relatively insubstantial character in the play, Lorenzo is fit both dramaturgically and morally to become the expositor of the doctrine of heaven's music. Dramaturgically, because Shakespeare must keep other characters who are more obviously eligible for the role—Bassanio, Portia, and Antonio—in reserve for the next stage of dramatic revelations. The playwright must guard against anticlimax: after this dramatically and thematically crucial musical moment, there is still the business of the rings to deal with. The joke of the rings—another "trick" by which a wonder suggestive of miracle is made to seem familiar—is begun in Venice at the end of act 4; now the audience must be kept interested in the present stage-moment and simultaneously in suspense as it awaits the wind-up of that joke. Lorenzo, therefore, is from the technical point of view an excellent expedient.

His moral fitness has also been established. Shakespeare has made us confident of the honest worthiness of Lorenzo's love for Jessica; that confidence, earlier established, is crucial for our response to the teasing banter at the opening of the fifth act. In the scene of their elopement (2.6), Gratiano (who accompanies Lorenzo) had praised Jessica with a typically insouciant pun—but one which, like his puns that close the play, carries a greater weight than Gratiano may intend: "Now (by my hood) a *gentle,* and no Jew" (2.6.51: where "gentle" is to be heard also as *Gentile*). And Lorenzo replies:

> Beshrew me but I love her heartily,
> For she is wise, if I can judge of her,
> And fair she is, if that mine eyes be true,
> And true she is, as she hath prov'd herself:
> And therefore like herself, wise, fair, and true,
> Shall she be placed in my constant soul.
>
> [2.6.52–57]

This rhetorically elaborate little encomium serves to fill up the time it takes Jessica to "make fast the doors and gild [herself] / With some moe ducats, and be with [Lorenzo] straight" (2.6.49–50). But other words than those Lorenzo uses would have served that technical purpose equally well. Shakespeare has chosen to enlighten this dark scene of their stealing away with the bright language of love.

Lorenzo's declaration "I love her heartily" is followed by the reasons for his love—and appropriately the fact that "she is wise" is first in order. That Jessica is also "fair" (the next quality mentioned) we have no reason to doubt, but Lorenzo is scrupulous to add "if that mine eyes be true." And then, weaving his eyes' truth into the truth of Jessica's moral character, Lorenzo concludes, "And true she is, as she hath prov'd herself." Finally, Jessica's qualities become the guiding principles for Lorenzo's own conduct: "And therefore like herself, wise, fair, and true, / Shall she be placed in my constant soul." The constancy of Lorenzo's soul is thus guaranteed by the virtuous features—wise, fair, and true—Jessica brings to it.

The fact that Jessica also brings a generous supply of Shylock's ducats complicates but does not contradict Lorenzo's claim. Part of that complication is of our own modern making, the result of our difficulty in seeing without disjunction both the relatively "realistic" and the parabolic aspects of Shakespeare's art. This union of the Gentile husband and the daughter of the Jew suggests the penultimate stage of salvation-history described by St. Paul: "Haue they [i.e., the Jews] stombled, that they sholde fall? God forbid: but through their fall saluation commeth vnto the Gentiles, to prouoke them to follow them. / Wherefore if the fall of them be the riches of the worlde, & the diminishing of them the riches of the Gentiles, how much more shal their abundance be?" (Rom. 11 : 11–12). Gilding herself with her father's ducats, Jessica is in process of transforming the fool's gold of this world, that "hard fare for Midas," into the spiritual gold of salvation. Shylock's rigid adherence to a literal law was a stumbling block of his own devising; his "diminishing" became "the riches of the Gentiles"—and then, through Antonio's merciful gesture after the court has rendered its verdict, a still greater abundance passes to Jessica, the "Gentile Jew." [5] This is the last of the play's revelations, a final blessing, made after the rings have been returned and the news given that Antonio's argosies are "richly come to harbour suddenly." Portia redirects our attention on stage: "How now Lorenzo? / My clerk hath some good comforts too for you" (5.1.288–89). And Nerissa speaks:

> Ay, and I'll give them him without a fee.
> There do I give to you and Jessica
> From the rich Jew, a special deed of gift
> After his death, of all he dies possess'd of.
> [5.1.290–93]

Lorenzo's reply appropriately accepts the good news of a New Dispensation with imagery that encompasses the Old: "Fair ladies, you drop manna in the way / Of starved people" (5.1.294–95).

The scene (2.6) in which Lorenzo steals away with Jessica and the troublesome ducats follows immediately the scene in which Shylock, having been "bid forth to supper," goes "in hate, to feed upon / The prodigal Christian" (2.5.14–15). Shylock begins with a promise to Launcelot, who for his own reasons is about "To leave a rich Jew's service, to become / The follower" of a Christian (2.2.140–41); Shylock says: "Well, thou shalt see, thy eyes shall be thy judge, / The difference of old Shylock and Bassanio" (2.5.1–2). Thus the arch-literalist puts us on notice—even the emphasis on judging by the eyes is significant—that these scenes of leave-takings (Shylock goes to supper, Jessica goes to Lorenzo, Bassanio to Portia) will distinguish between the principles embodied in the old Jewish father and the young Christian lovers.

The glimpse we get of Shylock's home life in 2.5 has con-

5. Cf., Lewalski, "Biblical Allusion," p. 343; Fisch, *Dual Image*, pp. 14–15.

vinced some that Shylock is "sober rather than miserly in his domestic life, and filled with the idea of the sanctity of the family and family loyalty." [6] But that is certainly *not* what Shakespeare's carefully contrived juxtapositions imply. We have listened already to Shylock's reaction to the impending masque and its music (2.5.28–36, 50–54): his warning to Jessica to "lock up my doors," his description of the masquers' music as "vile squealing," his condemnation of the celebrants as "fools with varnish'd faces." He has demanded specifically that Jessica "stop my house's ears," that she "shut doors," since "fast bind, fast find [is] / A proverb never stale in thrifty mind." And though the planned masque does not, in fact, take place, we have good reason not to trust either his musical or his moral criticism. Precisely because his idea of a "sober house" is that it be locked and shuttered, a dark silent vault for the treasures of the earth, Shylock convicts himself of being one of those to whom "God hathe giuen . . . the spirit of slomber: eyes that they shulde not se, & ears that they shulde not heare vnto this day" (Romans 11 : 8). What to Shylock's wilfully deaf ears is "vile squealing" and "shallow fopp'ry" is, in another scale, the joyful noise made by open-hearted "prodigals."

Shylock will hear no music, and he will "have no speaking" (3.3.17). He boasts that he is unyielding "to Christian intercessors" (3.3.16). He is fast bound behind the doors of that house which to Jessica "is hell" (2.3.2). It is inevitable, then, that Shylock will perceive around him only "fools with varnish'd faces." But when Jessica descends from the shuttered house to be Lorenzo's "torch-bearer," the revelry is seen by us in a more adequate way. This topsy-turvy night in Venice, with its disguisings, its gilding and stealing and hurried departures, and overall its young love, leads to Belmont's night; there we find, not the deafness of the Jew's

6. Graham Midgley, "*The Merchant of Venice:* A Reconsideration," p. 122.

house, but a "soft stillness" that admits "touches of sweet harmony."

Shakespeare chose not to present on stage Shylock's discovery of Jessica's flight. Instead he allows Solanio and Salerio—notoriously unreliable reporters—to mediate our experience. Their version of what "the dog Jew did utter in the streets" is indeed calculated to draw a laugh. It appeals to just the kind of ugly crowd reaction which they themselves describe: "Why all the boys in Venice follow him, / Crying his stones, his daughter, and his ducats" (2.8.23–24).[7] Now Shakespeare could have presented Shylock's reaction directly, had it been to his purpose; among other things he had the example of Marlowe, who gives directly to his Jew of Malta lines which, like Shylock's reported outcry, comically confuse his daughter with his gold. Indeed Barabas' lines are more ingeniously confused than those Solanio reports. In Barabas' summary line, "Oh girl, oh gold, oh beauty, oh my bliss!" (*Malta* 2.1.58), it really is impossible to say whether that final "bliss" refers to the girl or the gold. Barabas' entire speech is more controlled, the ironic conflation of disparates is more pointed, the satire is in every way more direct than in Solanio's speech. And this difference between Shakespeare's version and Marlowe's points up their essentially different artistic aims. In Barabas' speech the satire is aimed directly at the speaker, who is the Jew; in Solanio's speech the satire is also aimed at the speaker—but he is a Christian *acting* (better, perhaps, than he intends) the part of a merciless Jew. The relative crudeness of Solanio's mimicry, in other words, cuts in two directions, forcing us toward a complicated response simultaneously to the Jew and to the Christian mediator:

> I never heard a passion so confus'd,
> So strange, outrageous, and so variable

7. Stoll's basic mistake in his influential *Shakespeare Studies* is, in effect, to accept a Salerio-Solanio point of view as though it were indistinguishable from Shakespeare's own.

As the dog Jew did utter in the streets,—
"My daughter! O my ducats! O my daughter!
Fled with a Christian! O my Christian ducats!
Justice, the law, my ducats, and my daughter!
A sealed bag, two sealed bags of ducats,
Of double ducats, stol'n from me by my daughter!
And jewels, two stones, two rich and precious stones,
Stol'n by my daughter! Justice!—find the girl,
She hath the stones upon her, and the ducats!"

[2.8.12–22]

We recognize in this a good deal of the Shylock we know: in moments of crisis Shylock's cry will always be for "justice" and "the law"; and in a later scene we will actually hear him, speaking more savagely even than in the Solanio version, yoking Jessica with the jewels: "I would my daughter were dead at my foot, and the jewels in her ear: would she were hears'd at my foot, and the ducats in her coffin" (3.1.80–83).

But for all we hear of Shylock in Solanio's speech, we hear also the pleasure Solanio takes in reporting the Jew's discomfiture. By his mocking the literal Jew, Solanio exposes his own malice, his own lack of charity. Thus Shakespeare complicates the joy we may feel at Jessica's escape by alloying it, not only with sorrow for Shylock's destructive self-enclosure, but also with Solanio's unwitting reminder that Shylock is hardly alone in his spiritual tone-deafness. That latter reminder is an important aspect of Shakespeare's realism.

In act 5, Lorenzo calls for music specifically because Portia, mistress of the house, is approaching:

Come ho! and wake Diana with a hymn,
With sweetest touches pierce your mistress' ear,
And draw her home with music.

[66–68]

We recall Portia's own words on the triumphal associations of musical harmony: if Bassanio chooses the right casket, she has said,

> Then music is
> Even as the flourish, when true subjects bow
> To a new-crowned *monarch:* such it is,
> As are those dulcet sounds in break of day,
> That creep into the dreaming bridegroom's ear,
> And summon him to *marriage.*
>
> [3.2.48–53]

Music is thus doubly appropriate to Portia's homecoming. As mistress of the house, she is the "monarch" of Belmont's microcosmic realm, and deserving of "the flourish." Moreover, her wedding to Bassanio, though it had been celebrated in church, has not been consummated in bed. News of Antonio's distress intervened, and Portia had dispatched Bassanio to Venice "to pay the petty debt"—"For never shall you lie by Portia's side / With an unquiet soul" (3.2.304–06). For all three of the play's wedded couples, the music of act 5 retains its epithalamic associations.

The gently teasing quality of the Jessica-Lorenzo dialogue has been heard by us even before its most notable use at the opening of act 5. Because their dialogue will go on to describe most explicitly the doctrine of divine harmony, it is essential that we be accustomed to their sophisticated lovers' speech, which accommodates both easy bantering and serious intimacy. In the third act we hear this flexibility of tone in Jessica's speech praising Portia and in Lorenzo's reply to it:

> *Jessica.* It is very meet
> The Lord Bassanio live an upright life,
> For having such a blessing in his lady
> He finds the joys of heaven here on earth,
> And if on earth he do not merit it,
> In reason he should never come to heaven!

Why, if two gods should play some heavenly match,
And on the wager lay two earthly women,
And Portia one, there must be something else
Pawn'd with the other, for the poor rude world
Hath not her fellow.
Lorenzo. Even such a husband
Hast thou of me, as she is for a wife.
Jessica. Nay, but ask my opinion too of that.
Lorenzo. I will anon,—first let us go to dinner.
Jessica. Nay, let me praise you while I have a stomach.
Lorenzo. No pray thee, let it serve for table-talk,
Then howsome'er thou speak'st, 'mong other things
I shall digest it.

[3.5.67–84]

There is a delicacy here that is missing from Gratiano's capering. In its wittily domestic familiarity, the distinctive Jessica-Lorenzo tone of voice is able to carry the serious aspect of Jessica's encomium—that Bassanio finds in Portia heavenly joys here on earth; and simultaneously to give a delightful flesh-and-blood dwelling to these lofty thoughts of love.

So when Lorenzo, in act 5, modulates to a more grave, sententious tone of voice there is no sense of incongruity. Launcelot Gobbo has, for a moment, erupted onto the scene, bellowing news of Bassanio's approach. Now, alone with Jessica again, Lorenzo begins by reestablishing for the audience a nocturnal perception of the scene—and in such a way as to make us ever grateful for the technological poverty of the Shakespearean stage:

How sweet the moonlight sleeps upon this bank!
Here will we sit, and let the sounds of music
Creep in our ears—soft stillness and the night
Become the touches of sweet harmony:
Sit Jessica,—

[5.1.54–58]

And because Jessica is a newcomer, and because he loves her, Lorenzo tells Jessica about the musical wonders of this peaceful night:

> look how the floor of heaven
> Is thick inlaid with patens of bright gold:
> There's not the smallest orb which thou behold'st
> But in his motion like an angel sings,
> Still quiring to the young-ey'd cherubins;
> Such harmony is in immortal souls,
> But whilst this muddy vesture of decay
> Doth grossly close it in, we cannot hear it.
>
> [5.1.58–65]

Lorenzo's pedagogical tact is demonstrated as much by what he does not say as by what he does. The modern scholar can direct us to various sources for the ideas contained in Lorenzo's speech. But within the play itself the venerable traditions that validate the speech are felt in the very gravity and clarity of the speech's manner.

Still, since the modern reader or auditor is even less familiar with these ideas than is Jessica, some guidance is in order. Beginning with the lexical: though most of the recent editions widely used by students gloss the word "patens" in such a way as to leave them merely decorative blotches against the night sky, the word has, in fact, a specifically sacramental association.[8] These "patens of bright gold" to which Lorenzo likens the stars refer (as the note in the Arden edition explains) to "shallow dishes, as used in

8. Here are the footnotes provided for the reader in some widely-accepted collected editions: The Signet Shakespeare: *patens* = "tiles"; Hardin Craig / David Bevington: "thin, circular plates of metal"; Pelican: "metal plates or tiling"; Riverside: "metal plates or discs." A welcome exception is W. Moelwyn Merchant's edition for the New Penguin Shakespeare: *patens* is there glossed as "the dish, of silver or gold, from which the consecrated bread of the eucharist is served." The suppression of the sacramental associations of the word, in a passage

the celebration of the Holy Communion." We will also want to know that a congeries of ideas with good pagan foundations is made explicitly Christian in Lorenzo's version. Cicero's influential *Somnium Scipionis* (as it is preserved in Macrobius' commentary) talks about heavenly music; but for man's inability to hear that music, Cicero explains that we are deafened "like those who live too near the cataracts of the Nile." [9] Lorenzo, however, alludes to "man's fallen state: our senses are clogged by the grossness of our flesh" (Heninger, p. 5); and thus, while enclosed in the muddy vesture of mortality, we retain only an intimation of the celestial music accessible to the pure spirit.

When Jessica, with (I take it) a newcomer's insecurity, confesses "I am never merry when I hear sweet music"—and Lorenzo replies reassuringly, "The reason is your spirits are attentive"—it is worth knowing that her properly attuned listening attitude reflects the widely known doctrine of Boethius. According to Boethius, whose *De Institutione Musica* "remained an unquestioned authority on the music of Antiquity and on music in general for a thousand years after its composition in the early sixth century," there are three interrelated types of music: *musica mundana, musica humana,* and *musica instrumentalis.*[10] The first term refers to the music produced by the wondrous order of the cosmos itself; the second, "human music," is " 'that which unites the incorporeal activity of the reason with the body . . . a certain mutual adaptation and as it were tempering of high and low sounds into a single consonance' " (Hollander, p. 25). Where there is *musica humana,* there is in the individual a harmonious blending of soul and body, reason

too likely to be dismissed as just so much pretty "poetry" in any case, is a serious one.

9. Quoted in S. K. Heninger, Jr., *Touches of Sweet Harmony: Pythagorean Cosmology and Renaissance Poetics* (San Marino, California, 1974), p. 5. I am indebted to Heninger for other parts of this discussion.

10. I quote Hollander, *Untuning of the Sky,* p. 25.

and passion; and that personal harmony is analogous to the harmony of the cosmos (at one extreme) and the tuning of the strings of a musical instrument (at the other extreme).

We are likely to think of "human music" as being an attribute only of the emotions; its relation to the *reason* should therefore be stressed. In the Boethian system, the effects of music are moral and intellectual.

> The origin of music, Boethius tells us in *De Arithmetica,* is God Himself, and his means of creating it is exemplarism from the unchanging laws of number in His mind. From these laws are drawn the relations of the elements, of the seasons, and of the stars . . . and by means of these laws, *the intellectual role of . . . music* is to lead man's mind from the deceiving senses back to certain *knowledge.*[11]

Therefore, in *The Merchant of Venice,* music properly accompanies Bassanio's casket-choice; it properly is called upon to draw home Portia and Nerissa; and it properly suggests itself as the accompaniment to the tripartite dance of gracious giving that unites Bassanio, Portia, and Antonio. And, of course, it confirms the difference between the play's two merchants: Antonio, who is out-of-tune as the play opens but is attuned when he extends his love beyond the circle of his friends; and Shylock, who wilfully prefers his silent entombment in the flesh.

The intellectual history of the ideas out of which Lorenzo's speech on celestial music is made—its Platonic and Pythagorean bases, its Roman and Christian elaborations, its presence in the works of Shakespeare's contemporaries: this history, embarrassingly rich, is of intrinsic interest. But it is not necessary to dwell on it in order to appreciate the

11. David S. Chamberlain, "Philosophy of Music in the *Consolatio* of Boethius," *Speculum,* 45 (1970): 81. This worthwhile addition to the account available in Hollander was brought to my attention by Professor D. W. Robertson, Jr.; my italics.

speech, so tactful is Lorenzo's pedagogy. Of the moral effects of musical harmony, for instance, Lorenzo says that there is

> naught so stockish, hard, and full of rage
> But music for the time doth change his nature,—
> The man that hath no music in himself,
> Nor is not moved with concord of sweet sounds,
> Is fit for treasons, stratagems, and spoils;
> The motions of his spirit are dull as night,
> And his affections dark as Erebus:
> Let no such man be trusted.
>
> [5.1.81–88]

Lorenzo's treatment of music's role in human and in cosmic nature is at once description and demonstration: it enacts its meanings. It leaves us, as audience, as it does Jessica, prepared to "mark the music."

The task of establishing the harmony that the stockish Shylock would like to silence is not left entirely to Lorenzo, however. It is begun immediately after the trial, before we reach Belmont, by Portia herself; and in Belmont it will be continued by her. When the grateful Bassanio and Antonio attempt (at the Duke's suggestion) to "gratify this gentleman," the wise young judge, "For in my mind you are much bound to him" (4.1.403), the disguised Portia is able to prepare for the culminating comic trial, the test of the rings. And as she does so she is able to bring to single focus much of the play's dominant imagery, including that of indebtedness, gift-giving, and mercy's deeds; of learning and teaching; of the circle of charity, and the harmony of wedded love.

From Seneca's *De Beneficiis,* we recall that "the man who, when he gives, has any thought of repayment deserves to be deceived" (Loeb ed., p. 7). The recipient, however, is *obliged* to repay, since "a benefit passing in its course from hand to hand [must return] to the giver [since] the beauty of the whole is destroyed if the course is anywhere broken" (p. 15). When Bassanio and Gratiano attempt to repay the lawyer to whom they are "much bound," therefore, and that sly lawyer rebuffs the attempted recompense, they discover potential pitfalls for those who would dance in the ring of the Graces. Two apparently irreconcilable obligations—that the giver give freely but that the recipient repay—are among the elements Shakespeare uses to create the play's final dilemma, out of which he will bring its final comic resolution.

Shakespeare begins by reintroducing the language of commerce and calculation, as Bassanio tries literally to repay measure for measure:

> Most worthy gentleman, I and my friend
> Have by your wisdom been this day acquitted
> Of grievous penalties, in lieu whereof,
> Three thousand ducats due unto the Jew
> We freely cope your courteous pains withal.
>
> [4.1.404–08]

First it was Shylock who had refused the three thousand ducats; now it is Shylock's judge:

> *Portia.* He is well paid that is well satisfied,
> And I delivering you, am satisfied,
> And therein do account myself well paid,—
> My mind was never yet more mercenary.
>
> [411–14]

Perhaps the lesson of the courtroom has not been sufficiently learned; perhaps less punctilious men would accept this declaration that the debt has already been paid: at any rate, Bassanio insists upon making further payment, insists that some *tangible* benefit pass from hand to hand. And thus, through his own insisting, Bassanio gets himself out of the frying pan into the fire:

Portia. You press me far, and therefore I will yield,—
Give me your gloves, I'll wear them for your sake,
And (for your love) I'll take this ring from you,—
Do not draw back your hand, I'll take no more,
And you in love shall not deny me this!
[4.1.421–25]

An audience may not recall, as Portia speaks these lines, the terms in which Shylock originally made the nearly-fatal loan—but the characters, as well as the actors and the attentive reader, should:

To *buy* his favor, I extend this *friendship,*—
If he will take it, so,—if not, adieu,
And for my *love* I pray you wrong me not.
[1.3.164–66]

In Shylock's wickedly playful lines, *buying* balances *friendship,* and the word *love* clinches the deal. At the end of act 4 it is Portia's turn to urge "love" (twice in the lines I have quoted) to seal the problematic transaction.

The verbal echo, which casts us back to that dangerous world where love and commerce make such an unstable compound, is the first of several by which Portia makes this final comic trial an echo of the trial just passed. In her attitude as a whole, which changes from a courteous disregard for payment into a Shylockian implacability, and in details of language, she unsettles Bassanio (while delighting the audience which is privy to the joke) by seeming to return him to the harsh arena of the law.

Shylock's passion for "justice" had been a mechanism to silence the humanizing voice: "I'll have no speaking, I will have my bond" (3.3.17). In his short scene with Antonio and the gaoler, the reiterated "I'll have my bond" apparently sealed the play on a tragic course. Now, as Portia begins the trial's comic reprise, she assumes the Shylockian pose: to

Bassanio's embarrassed protestation, "This ring, good sir? alas it is a trifle, / I'll not shame myself to give you this," she replies, "I will have nothing else but only this, / And now methinks I have a mind to it!" (4.1.426–29). And when Bassanio pleads, "There's more depends on this than on the value . . . Only for this I pray you pardon me," Portia's reply again echoes Shylock: "You taught me first to beg" she says; "and now methinks / You teach me how a beggar should be answered" (435–36). This echo the audience may well be expected to hear; it recalls the perverse lesson Shylock drew from the acknowledging of a common humanity, that "The villainy *you teach me* I will execute, and it shall go hard but I will better the instruction" (3.1.65–66).

Bassanio tries to protect the ring with a clear statement of its special value as a pledge of loving loyalty:

> Good sir, this ring was given me by my wife,
> And when she put it on, she made me vow
> That I should neither sell, nor give, nor lose it.
> [4.1.437–39]

Portia's response serves as another comic turn of the screw—"That 'scuse serves many men to save their gifts," she says—and as an oblique reminder of the universal obligation to an openness in giving:

> And if your wife be not a mad-woman,
> And know how well I have deserv'd this ring,
> She would not hold out enemy for ever
> For giving it to me: well, peace be with you!
> [4.1.441–44]

Portia's ring must be given in order that charity be kept; formally and thematically it is the counterpoise to Leah's ring. And as Portia goes off with Nerissa, she leaves Antonio—the openhanded merchant of the play's first free gift—to urge the necessity for letting the ring go:

> My Lord Bassanio, let him have the ring,
> Let his deservings and my *love* withal
> Be valued 'gainst your wife's *commandement.*
> [445–47]

But in the same instant the comic trap is set, as Antonio unthinkingly makes "love" the antagonist of "commandement," and as an act of generosity once again sets Mercy in opposition to Justice.

The courtroom trial had been a drawn out affair; this final comic trial is correspondingly brief—tightly wound up at the end of act 4, and then quickly unwound at the play's conclusion. By the time of Portia's entrance in act 5, "soft stillness and the night" have almost passed; it is now an ambiguous moment, neither night nor yet fully day:

> This night methinks is but the daylight sick,
> It looks a little paler,—'tis a day,
> Such as the day is when the sun is hid.
> [5.1.124–26]

Portia's precision in describing this transitional moment is appropriately aimed at an audience awaiting the dawning of comic revelations. The jarring new note Portia brings into the musical scene—a "cuckoo"-voice (as she acknowledges it) of ribald teasing—is also appropriate. The men will be made to squirm for a few moments before sexual anxiety gives way to sexual love.

The ribaldry is carried in part by the punning that now becomes so notable an aspect of the dialogue. And the punning, too, is appropriate, for the pun can be a most generous rhetorical figure, yielding double linguistic value on the word. Portia's first words to Bassanio as she enters are in the common quibbling coin of Elizabethan comedy: "Let me give light, but let me not be light, / For a light wife doth make a heavy husband" (129–30). The play on "heavy" (that is, *sad* but also *weighty* with a cuckold's horns), and on "light" (which, in addition to its sexual sense, carries on the idea of the candle that shines like "a good deed in a naughty world" [5.1.89–91]), continues the punning vein begun in her description of the time—which is "sick" because "it looks a little paler."

It would be labor lost to sum up a play as rich as *The Merchant of Venice* with a single rhetorical figure or flourish. It will always "exceed account." In its smallest details of action and language the play's final scene simultaneously sounds a satisfyingly resolving chord and carries its musical suggestiveness beyond the reach of discursive language. When Portia, for instance, pretends to chastise Gratiano for the loss of Nerissa's ring, she reminds him that it was "riveted with faith unto your flesh" (5.1.169), and that her own husband, Bassanio, would not have given away his ring "for the wealth / That the world masters" (173–74). Like the pun, such lines as these generously yield more than face value. The audience, from its privileged perspective, is allowed to have both the comedy of sexual intrigue and the more divine comedy in which Portia's words carry so much weight because their literal functions are fulfilled in spiritual truths. Portia's threatenings are converted and gentled by their quibbling suggestiveness, their contextual richness:

> Since he ["Balthazar"] hath got the jewel that I loved,
> And that which you did swear to keep for me,
> I will become as liberal as you,
> I'll not deny him anything I have,
> No, not my body, nor my husband's bed:
> Know him I shall, I am well sure of it.
>
> [5.1.224–29]

Her taunting recalls Shylock's worldly anxiety: "Lie not a night from home," she warns; "watch me like Argus" (230). Only now there is available an efficacious language of pardon.

It is spoken by Bassanio: "Pardon this fault, and by my

soul I swear / I never more will break an oath with thee" (247–48). But unaided man could never achieve such rigorous perfection; as this very episode of the rings demonstrates, even the dictates of charity can be fulfilled only through the mutuality urged in Portia's version of the Lord's Prayer: "We do pray for mercy, / And that same prayer doth teach us all to render / The deeds of mercy." So again Antonio comes to Bassanio's aid, speaking now a language of newly revitalized legalism:

> I once did lend my body for his wealth,
> Which but for him that had your husband's ring
> Had quite miscarried. I dare be bound again,
> My soul upon the forfeit, that your lord
> Will never more break faith advisedly.
>
> [5.1.249–53]

Portia therefore first gives the ring to Antonio, who gives it in turn to Bassanio.

The revelations are made—leaving "all amaz'd" (266). Portia promises further explanations; and that promise, for one last time, nicely balances the realms of law and spirit: "Let us go in, / And charge us there upon inter'gatories, / And we will answer all things faithfully" (297–99). And then, in Gratiano's conclusive pun, "Well, while I live, I'll fear no other thing / So sore, as keeping safe Nerissa's ring," the letter is again fulfilled in the spirit, as a comic faith is confirmed by the fleshly and the golden ring.

Index

germ, circ
MONTGOMERY COLLEGE LIBRARIES
The harmonies
PR 2825.D3
0 0000 00178718 3